DUMBEST CRIMINALS

compiled by Wendy Lewis

NEW
HOLLAND

First published in Australia in 2005 by
New Holland Publishers (Australia) Pty Ltd
Sydney • Auckland • London • Cape Town

Unit 1/66 Gibbes St, Chatswood NSW 2067
218 Lake Road Northcote Auckland New Zealand
86 Edgware Road London W2 2EA United Kingdom
80 McKenzie Street Cape Town 8001 South Africa

10 9 8 7 6 5 4 3 2
National Library of Australia Cataloguing-in-Publication Data:

Dumbest criminals.
    ISBN 9781741102857
    1. Criminals - Humor. 2. Crime - Humor. I. Lewis, Wendy.
    364.3

Publisher: Fiona Schultz
Editor: Monica Berton
Designer: Greg Lamont
Cover Design: Karl Roper
Production Manager: Olga Dementiev
Printer: Publisher's Graphics

Stories in this book have been reproduced with kind permission from
www.dumbcriminalacts.com and www.dumbcrooks.com.

CONTENTS

INTRODUCTION

If you believe the movies, most criminals are cunning masterminds who drive around in fancy cars surrounded by a constantly changing bevy of beautiful companions. They love international travel, expensive clothes, and they live in high-security mansions overlooking the sea on some remote yet picturesque Caribbean island. Of course, they are also ruggedly good-looking (if they are a man), or slinky and sexy and shapely in Armani evening wear (if they are a woman). They are immaculately groomed, wear dazzling jewellery and drink fabulous cocktails on their sun-drenched terraces. These criminals are never caught; they have sophisticated communications systems and even more sophisticated stashes of weapons. They mock police and cause high-level embarrassment at every echelon of government. They zip in and out of international airports unseen, they laugh at danger, flaunt their success and lead fabulous lives of untold wealth, excitement and glamour. Hmm.

The reality, however, is a little different. Sorry to say, most modern-day criminals pale in comparison. And, although it would be nice to think otherwise, most heists are carried out by young male repeat offenders who don't know the first thing about what they're trying to do. They are unsophisticated and unprofessional and hardly able to cheat at cards, let alone get the better of a major institution such as a bank.

Figures show that 76 per cent of bank robbers don't use a disguise, despite the widespread use of surveillance cameras. Eighty-six per cent never study the bank before robbing it, and 95 per cent make no long-range plans for concealing the loot once it's in their hands. It's laughable that they even think for one moment that they could commit a crime successfully.

But this is what the book is about — small-time crims that make you wince, cringe and laugh. You'll discover criminals that will astound you with their stupidity, their clumsiness, and their pathetic attempts to quietly slip away from a heist gone wrong. Here's to you, dumb crooks of the world!

SHEER STUPIDITY

*Thieves and other criminals who
forgot that actions have consequences ...*

For starters, here are some classic stories of great criminal minds who just don't get it. You'll meet robbers, counterfeiters, kidnappers and plain old drunks who are not all there in the brain cell department — like the car thieves who stole a manual car when they both only drove automatics, or the fruitcake who decided to rob a casino over the phone! People like this make you feel proud to have an IQ over 40. They don't seem to realise that to get away with a crime you need to have a plan, you need to remain anonymous and, most importantly, you don't want the police to catch you. The only relevant advice to those contemplating a life of crime is — think it through, dumbo!

LOOK EVERYONE, THAT'S US!

A ram-raider gang reversed a stolen Saab into an exclusive department store and took photographs of themselves wearing expensive designer clothes before making their getaway. They wanted to show friends in prison how well they were doing—little did they know they were soon to see their friends on the inside again. They sent their happy snaps to the store they'd just raided for processing and were recognised instantly!

GUNS CAN BE DANGEROUS!

A budding young bandit decided to have a go at armed robbery. He chose a gun shop full of gun-loving customers to commit the crime. There was also a marked police car parked outside, but he didn't seem to notice, and the police officer happened to be one of the customers inside the shop. As the young man approached the counter and saw the police officer, he realised things weren't going exactly to plan, so he fired a few wild shots in the air. The police officer promptly returned fire and the doomed bandit was smartly marched out the door.

BIG BANG THEORY

A man decided to commit suicide. He brought a tank of propane, settled down onto his couch, opened the stop and waited to die. Instead of dying, he merely lost consciousness. Four hours later he revived and, forgetting the suicide attempt, he lit a cigarette. The violent explosion that followed blew out his apartment wall. Fortunately—or perhaps unfortunately—he survived.

SAY IT WITH DIAMONDS

A well-dressed, love-struck young man walked into a jewellery store on Valentine's Day and asked to look at a couple of diamond rings. While the assistant was getting one of the rings from a locked case, the guy snaffled an engagement ring and two wedding bands into his pocket and hightailed it out of there.

Of course, our Romeo had pure motives. A couple of days later, he got down on bended knee, proposed to his girlfriend, and presented her with two extremely valuable rings. She blissfully accepted, but her happiness was short-lived—the rings didn't fit her finger! Her senseless young suitor instantly thought of the most obvious and stupidest solution to her dilemma and told her she could just take them back to the jewellery store and have them re-sized.

When the poor dear walked in with her request, a shop assistant recognised the rings, told her to pick them up tomorrow, and then called the police.

WE CAN SEE YOU!

Police raided a printer's shop where they found $320 000 in counterfeit money. It was all laid out neatly in uncut sheets of $20 bills stacked in five or six piles. Police were suspicious of the operations of the shop for some time because it happened to be next door to the police station. In the end, they really appreciated how easy it had been to carry out surveillance!

DRUNK TAKES A DUNK

In a one-cop town in the Arctic Circle, the only access to the outside world is Alaska Airlines. When a plane is landing or taking off, there are large gates with flashing lights, like a railroad crossing, that come down and keep pedestrians and vehicles off the runway.

One afternoon the only policeman in town was called to respond to reports of an intoxicated male staggering around on the runway. The story began when the plane was due for take-off. It taxied to the end of the runway near the road and the gates came down complete with attention-grabbing flashing lights. However, being in a less then alert state, our drunken hero walked right past the flashing lights and through the gates.

By this stage the jet had turned around and was getting ready to begin its take-off down the runway when an official advised the pilot that there was a drunk standing behind the engines. The pilot waited for about 10 minutes and, after not hearing another word, assumed the human obstruction had gone. He hit the throttles to take off. Well, our inebriated trespasser was not out of the way and had apparently paused for a breather directly behind the jet to enjoy a whiff of those nice intoxicating exhaust fumes. He didn't stay long; he was picked up by the engine back blast and thrown into the air, clearing 10 metres of sandy beach and almost 20 metres of water before coming in for a 'splash down'. That lovely refreshing arctic water sure brought him round, enough for him to swim ashore and get arrested for trespassing ... and a few other things.

HEY, LET'S STEAL A POLICE CAR!

Two young men decided it would be a good idea to try and steal a police car and get themselves a shotgun. So, what did they do but break into a police security parking compound. They didn't realise that police don't leave lethal weapons in their vehicles, and it didn't occur to them that there would be security cameras taping them as they cut through the wire fence with bolt cutters. And, of course, being a high-security area, they were trapped like rats when several nearby officers responded to the call.

YOU JUST DON'T GET IT, DO YOU?

A not-too-bright prisoner was released on parole after serving a sentence for robbing a convenience store. The very day he was released, he went back to the same store, which is just two blocks from his house. He placed a paper bag over his hand—his hand, mind you, not his head—pretended to have a gun, and demanded money from the long-suffering shop assistant who knew the drill and even called him by his name. And, just to make things even easier for the police, the whole scene was caught on tape by the store's surveillance camera.

AND YOU'RE A WEEK BEHIND WITH THE RENT!

Out on bail for an armed robbery, a 35-year-old man just couldn't get enough of seeing the inside of a jail cell. He needed cash quickly and since he lived on top of a tavern, he decided that it would be an easy target. So he went downstairs, burst into the bar with a gun and demanded cash. The bartender handed it over to him and our fearless robber fled back upstairs. He was amazed when the police arrived five minutes later and found him sitting at the kitchen table, counting piles of money. In selecting his victim, he'd forgotten one thing—the bartender was his landlord!

ALPHA BRAVO CHARLIE?

A young woman suffering from a broken heart and a desire for revenge stabbed her ex-lover in the neck—which is a stupid thing to do at the best of times. But as it happens, she was on a Cessna plane in mid-air and her ex-lover happened to be the pilot. Fortunately, a passenger wrestled her to the ground and grabbed the knife from her. Her wounded ex managed to land the plane safely, but wisely decided not to take her on his next flight.

DON'T LEAVE THE
KEYS IN THE IGNITION!

On the last day of exams, three university students decided to play a prank by streaking through their local restaurant. Customers were quite amused to see them, but doubly amused to see a man finish his meal, leave the restaurant, get into their waiting car and drive off ... with all their clothes inside!

STRANGE AS IT SEEMS,
WE KNOWWHERE YOU ARE

Police didn't have much trouble tracking down a repeat offender who held-up two service stations. He was under house arrest at the time and was wearing a court-ordered electronic monitoring device.

NEXT TIME TAKE THE BUS!

A man went to pick up his wife from jail. The problem was that he stole a truck to do it and then parked in a specially marked disabled parking spot right across the street from police headquarters.

SMILE, YOU'RE ON CANDID CAMERA

Two armed robbers burst into a young Brazilian woman's home as she was using an Internet chat room. She was chatting with a friend in Uruguay, who saw what was happening and called a cousin who happened to live in Brazil in a town near his friend. The cousin then called the police. The ring-around was so quick that the officers reached the house in time to catch the robbers, who hadn't realised they had been captured on webcam.

WHAT DOES THIS PEDAL DO, SWEETIE?

A man and a woman approached another young woman outside a pub and at gunpoint demanded her car keys. She handed them over. The pair jumped into the car and jumped right out again ... neither of them could drive a manual!

PARK SOMEWHERE ELSE NEXT TIME

Two males and two females were discovered loading up their car with stolen furniture. It was a relatively easy arrest; they chose the police department parking lot to do it.

JUST GO!

An inmate successfully broke out of jail by scaling a three-metre chain-link fence. But instead of leaving the scene, he hung around and tried to hand a fellow inmate a cigarette through a steel grate covering the window. He was seen and arrested. Total time of freedom—nine minutes.

ANONYMOUS?

A long-time client of a tax agent went in to pick up his tax return. The clerk checked on the computer and told him that he would be getting his refund in the mail. That wasn't good enough. The client kicked up such a stink that he was sent through to the manager. At that point he drew a gun and demanded money. The manager calmly explained that they didn't have any money on the premises, and so our empty-handed friend ran away.

Looking at the scenario, what he did was pretty damn stupid. For a start, he was a client of the tax agency, so all his details were not hard to find ... all they had to do was look up his files on their computer. Secondly, there were six clients who witnessed the entire episode—from his initial outburst to the actual hold-up. And thirdly, as he left the premises, two young men were coming in and looked him right in the face. As a consequence, he was described perfectly by everyone there.

But there's more. When the police arrived at his place, he answered the door, wearing the same clothes, gun in hand. 'How did you find me?' he asked.

DO YOU READ ME? LOUD AND CLEAR!

A gang decided to use walkie-talkies to pull off their best heist ever. They were confident that the radios would allow them to monitor the police as well as coordinate their own activities. It never occurred to these mental athletes that the police might just be listening in ...

FROM THE COMFORT
OF YOUR OWN HOME

A not-too-bright fellow thought he would 'win' some money from a casino without leaving his house. He phoned a famous casino and demanded they deliver $100 000 or he would come to the casino and start shooting people. He gave them his home address for delivery purposes. Police gratefully received his details: 'It makes our job extremely easy when they give us their name and address.'

I'M FAMOUS!

Passers-by were bemused at a man who was standing in front of a shop window, pointing at a 'Wanted' poster taped to the glass. 'That's me!' he declared proudly to all, including two passing police officers.

BUDDY, CAN YOU SPARE $16?

A young man, who'd had a little bit too much to drink, tried to get change from a counterfeit $16 note. When a service station attendant refused to hand over cash to the young man, he threatened to call the police. 'Go ahead,' the attendant challenged him, and so he did. He was promptly arrested.

SHOW OFFS!

Two prison escapees wanted to win a prize for the best story-of-the-week on a local radio station. They reported their own escape, explaining how they had put a sleep-inducing drug into a guard's coffee before walking out of the prison. The radio station thought it was a great story. So did the police.

WE KNOW WHERE YOU ARE

A bungling burglar broke into a Mooney aircraft at a country airport and removed its avionics system, including the Emergency Locating Transmitter or ELT. This device sends homing signals if the aircraft crashes. You can guess what happened next. The ELT was accidentally activated—beep, beep, beep—and authorities had no trouble tracking down the crook.

CHECK THAT ADDRESS

A couple of rocket scientists were captured as they tried to break into someone's home in the middle of the night. The 'someone' who caught them was the police officer who lived there. He was impressed by the observational skills of the pair. They actually walked through his garage, right past his patrol car, before breaking into the house.

THAT'S WHAT YOU GET!

A young man stole $4000 from a parked car and then hitched a ride out of town. Once safely on his way, he began to tell the driver all about his heist. What he didn't count on was the driver pulling a gun, forcing him to hand over the cash and dumping him out of the car.

QUICK AS A FLASH

A young man robbed a convenience store by threatening the assistant with a knife. Problem was the shop assistant recognised him straight away—he worked in the sandwich shop next door. Added to the youth's ineptitude was the fact that the store was right opposite the local police station. Police arrived within 12 seconds.

WHAT A DUMMY

A nervous robber in a clothing shop grabbed a hostage ... who happened to be a shop mannequin. The gun-wielding robber threatened to shoot the life-like mannequin if the cops made any attempt to capture him. A police spokesperson said, 'He was either blind as a bat, stupid, or both'.

CAN'T KEEP AWAY

Three dumb inmates scaled a fence at a minimum-security prison at 2.00 am one Saturday morning. They threatened three people, hijacked their car, held-up a liquor store ... and then tried to sneak back into prison! The three men were picked up walking down a service road towards the prison an hour after their night-time escapade.

HAVE YOU THOUGHT
OF SOME OTHER CAREER?

A suspect in an armed robbery was arrested at his home. He was polite, non-violent, and absolutely dumbfounded about how the police could possibly have tracked him down. Turns out that he had recently applied for a job as a correctional officer in a state prison. Naturally, they ran a routine criminal background check ...

HI-TECH SET-UP

Realising that their suspect was not going to win the Nobel Prize for Intelligence, police interrogated a suspect by placing a metal colander on his head and connecting it with wires to a photocopier. They placed the message 'HE'S LYING' in the copier, and pressed the copy button each time they thought the suspect wasn't telling the truth. And wouldn't you know, believing the 'lie detector' was working, the suspect confessed.

AREN'T TEACHERS
SUPPOSED TO BE SMART?

A science teacher who didn't feel like teaching her regular 2.00 pm physics class rang the school and told them there was a bomb timed to go off at 2.00 pm. Five police officers and school staff searched the building but found nothing unusual. A few minutes later, she rang again to ask whether the physics class was going ahead ... that was enough for police to trace the calls to her. The principal told police she was a fine teacher with no prior criminal record, but no, she wouldn't be returning to work.

HOLD THE ANCHOVIES

Two men ordered a couple of pizzas and when the delivery guy arrived, they put a gun to his face. Reacting quickly, the delivery guy threw the pizzas at them, got back in his car and drove off. Police had no problem tracking down the pizza pilferers since they had ordered the pizzas giving their real names, phone number and address.

ER, HI MUM ...

Three teenagers attempted to rob a bus load of people without realising one of their mothers was sitting a few rows back. When she saw the driver threatened with knives and a baseball bat, she shouted at her son to behave himself and get off.

DON'T TASTE LIKE WHISKY TO ME, PARDNER

Thieves broke into a liquor store after closing one night and snatched six bottles of gin, bourbon and vodka. Forget about having a giant piss-up, boys ... they were display bottles filled with water and cold tea!

IF YOU WANT IT DONE WELL, DO IT YOURSELF!

A not-too-bright young man decided to holdup his neighbour at gunpoint. She told him she didn't have any cash so he got her to drive him to her nearest bank branch. He didn't really think through the next step. What happened was, he waited in the car while his neighbour went in to the bank supposedly to withdraw money for him. Naturally, she told the teller to call the police and the young man was surprised when a police officer—and not his neighbour—came knocking on the car window.

TRY A TAXI!

An intoxicated university student at a fast food outlet needed a ride home, so he came up with a truly stupid plan. He rang the police and made a bomb threat so that the police would show up, arrest him, and give him a lift. He didn't count on the 18-month prison sentence.

CAUGHT!

A young man had a little too much time on his hands one day and decided to play with a set of handcuffs he had lying around the house. He put them on and then realised he didn't have a key. So did he call a locksmith? No. He called the police.

The responding officers ran a routine computer check and found that their 'prisoner' had an outstanding warrant for his arrest. He was taken into custody wearing his own handcuffs. 'We took them off like he asked,' a police spokesperson later said, 'only he was in jail at the time.'

SLEEP TIGHT!

A man broke into a grocery store and in a stroke of genius decided to use a chainsaw to get into the store's safe. He was overcome by the carbon monoxide fumes belching from the saw's engine and was found by police five hours later unconscious on the floor.

THIRSTY WORK

A young man went into a hotel, pulled out a gun, and demanded money—which he got. Apparently this made him thirsty so he asked for a beer. The bar assistant told him he didn't look old enough and asked to see his ID. The crook obliged by pulling out his driver's licence. Then off he toddled, taking the cash and alcohol with him, as the assistant jotted down his name and address and called police. When he got back home there were two nice men in blue uniforms waiting for him.

HOLD THE TARTARE SAUCE

A man rushed into a fish and chip shop and ordered the lunchtime special. Nothing strange about that except that the man was completely out of breath, red in the face, sweating all over, and panting like a wounded dog. No wonder—he'd just held-up a bank! While the chips were frying, a description of him was being circulated and police officers apprehended him before he'd finished eating. Probably next time he should save lunch 'til he gets home.

SAFE AND SORRY?

As two cleaners left an exclusive restaurant early one morning, two robbers forced them back inside the restaurant at gunpoint, bound them with duct tape, and robbed them. They then dragged out the restaurant safe, loaded it into the boot of one of the cleaner's cars and headed off. That's when they hit the speed bump in the restaurant parking lot and the 80-kilogram safe tumbled out onto the road. What to do? They figured that the safe would open if they drove over it with the car, so they did, but the safe didn't open. The frustrated robbers tried again ... and again. You'd think that eventually they'd try something different but no, they kept on at it. They wreaked havoc on the poor stolen car, but the safe was barely dented.

Half and hour later, one of the cleaners finally freed himself and called police. When the police showed up, the men didn't even notice them ... they were still busy in the parking lot, totally preoccupied with trying to open that elusive safe.

HEAVY STUFF!

Around 3.00 a.m. on a hot sticky summer's morning, a man was awakened by the sound of a forklift truck. Furious that the timber yard next door was disturbing his sleep, he threw open the curtains only to find two guys attempting to steal a huge safe on a forklift.

One guy was working the forklift with the safe attached, while the other idiot was backing up in an old station wagon. Yep, you guessed it! He put the safe into the back of the car, started to lower the forklift, and sure enough, the car's back axle broke and the car was squashed. The second idiot was still gunning the engine trying to drive away in the broken car with the safe in it as three police cars pulled up. For the man looking out his window, it was a great evening's entertainment!

HEY DRIVER!

An escaped prisoner was recaptured on the first day of his new job. His choice of job was rather interesting—driving a bus—but not just any bus; a mini bus that takes friends and relatives to visit inmates in prison. As the police who captured him wondered: why would you escape from prison and then get a job where you drive into the prison every week?

HOW DID YOU PAY FOR THAT?

A security guard managed to disable security cameras for 30 minutes in the bank vault in the head office of his work during one lunchbreak. He then proceeded to walk out with $402 000 in cash. If only he had played it cool for a little while ... You see, he wasn't a suspect until he arrived at work the next day in a very expensive 2000 Chevrolet Corvette.

DOGGY DO, DOGGY DON'T!

Things can spiral out of control, as one young lady found out. One morning she was walking her dog and by lunchtime she was in jail wondering why she did what she did. It began when she went for a walk in the park with her dog. On the way home, a police officer stopped her to issue a fine for failing to clean up after her dog at an intersection. Instead of simply accepting the fine, the lady walked away from the police officer and refused to return, which resulted in a charge of obstructing justice. Then when she was taken into custody, she began to kick and shove the arresting officer ... and that's how she landed in jail. Oh, and what's more, they took her dog away.

IT'S A STEAL AT $50!

A man who had his sports utility vehicle stolen from a golf course was surprised to get a call over the weekend telling him he could have it back for $50. The man arranged to meet the mysterious caller at a liquor store to make the swap. He also arranged for some police to be on stand-by. When the man made contact with the owner, he was immediately arrested, which raises two interesting questions. Did he really think he would get away with it? And if he did, why didn't he ask for more than $50?

NICE VIEW OF YOUR REAR END!

Four guys in a pick-up truck attempted to steal an ATM by wrapping a logging chain around it, attaching it to the bumper of their truck, and pulling the entire ATM loose from its foundations. They failed to move it at all, but the little security camera inside the ATM got an excellent photo of the rear of the truck and its registration plate.

RAINDROPS KEEP FALLIN' ON MY HEAD

A young man who worked in the electrical department of a major London retail store couldn't contain his child-like curiosity ... and now he has plenty of time in a cell to be as curious as he likes. Despite his claims of innocence, he was caught on closed-circuit television, completely inebriated, looking suspiciously at the sprinkler system in a rival department store. Then he was clearly seen getting out a lighter and holding it up to the sprinkler system. The result? Thousands of litres of water gushing out of one sprinkler causing irreparable damage to over $1 million worth of stock in the home entertainment department including plasma TVs, videos, DVD players and stereo systems ...

EXCUSE ME, GET OFF MY CAR

A police officer was on patrol one Saturday night when he stopped his car at a stop sign. Two men were standing on the footpath arguing and suddenly started throwing punches at each other. They fell over and landed right on the hood of the officer's car and kept right on laying into each other even though he was sitting there, watching them through his windscreen. Several bystanders began laughing and cheering them on. The police officer then turned on his overhead lights and siren to try and attract their attention, but to no avail. Finally he got out of the car and pulled them apart with physical force. He was as embarrassed as they were ... but took them to jail anyway.

HAIRY FEET!

A peeping Tom hiding in the women's change room at a gym was caught after a woman in a neighbouring shower cubicle spotted him. She didn't exactly spot him, but she did spot his suspiciously hairy feet. The 43-year-old man was charged with six counts of indecent behaviour. Apparently he hid in a shower and used a small mirror to catch glimpses of showering and disrobing women, but he failed to conceal his hirsute tootsies.

DON'T I KNOW YOU?

When a masked man pointed a gun at a young lady behind the counter of an auto repair shop, she thought she recognised his voice. Police later realised it was quite likely because the man holding the gun happened to be her brother. Police established that the girl had no knowledge that her brother was planning the hold-up. Indeed, she helped track him down. While they were interviewing her after the robbery, her brother called. The police officer told her to stay on the line as long as she could and dispatchers traced the call to a nearby pay phone ... one brother apprehended!

PRETTY IN PINK!

A lady who worked in a toy store discovered that her locker at work had been broken into and her purse had been stolen. She had only recently bought a new ute and her car keys were inside. She went out to the parking lot and, sure enough, her ute was gone.

Two days later when she arrived at work, she was surprised to see her ute back in the store parking lot. The same make, same year, same numberplates ... but it had been painted bright pink! It turned out that the ute had been stolen by another employee at the toy store, who claimed that the real owner had told him she would let him drive the vehicle if he gave it a new paint job. The police didn't buy his story.

NOT THE BRIGHTEST
BULBS IN THE CLOSET

Two guys walked into a video store brandishing a knife and threatening to kill the employees if they didn't give them money. But one of the workers decided they looked pretty unsure of themselves, so despite the threat, he told the robbers that they didn't have any cash in the store. The two guys got mad, knocking all the stuff off the counter in a big temper tantrum, and then they left. The employees got a good look at their car—a red 1999 Honda Accord—and rang the police.

About an hour and a half later, the two employees feared for the worst when they saw the red Honda once again pull up outside the store. They began to panic as they watched the two hoons get out of their car, walk towards the entrance, kick open the door and ... ask for directions.

As the police officer who arrested them shortly after surmised: 'I guess they got lost. They're not the brightest bulbs in the closet.'

HELP ME, OFFICER!

In the middle of the night, a police patrol car stopped to assist a man at the side of the road who was having trouble starting his car. He said he was having engine problems and asked them to help push the car so he could start it up. But the police officers became suspicious when they saw the car's stereo on the front seat. They asked the man a simple question and realised they definitely had a thief on their hands— he didn't know the registration number of the vehicle.

IT'S THE THOUGHT THAT COUNTS

A young military recruit decided to impress his parents by sending them a 'war souvenir'. He carefully packed up his army-issue pistol and sent off the package to his parents. What caught the attention of the postal inspectors was that he had dutifully filled out the required customs declaration with complete honesty, stating that the package contained a pistol. Silly boy. He got a court martial for theft of government property.

POLICE ERROR

An off-duty police officer had a pistol-shaped cigarette lighter, which he had been using all night while drinking at a local tavern. After many hours and drinks, he mistook his .32 revolver for the lighter. When he went to light his cigarette, you guessed it—he shot the guy five stools away at the bar ...

CAN'T DO THAT, MA'AM

There is a small business called Guns for Hire, which stages gunfights for movies and hires out costumes and props. One day, they received a call from a 47-year-old woman who was very interested in their services. But, unfortunately, she had a mistaken idea about what they did. She wondered whether they could help because she wanted to have her husband bumped off.

KIDNAP CAPERS

The 21-year-old daughter of a media magnate was kidnapped, but don't worry about her fate, because let's say right at the start that the kidnappers were as thick as two planks. The kidnappers sent a photograph of their captive to her family. In the photograph she was holding a newspaper. However, it wasn't that day's edition, nor that year's edition, nor even that decade's edition! It bore a prominent headline relating to Nixon's trip to China. This was pointed out to the pea-brained abductors in a subsequent phone call. Miffed at being criticised, they determined to get it right the next time. So, they responded by sending a new photograph. The new photograph showed an up-to-date newspaper—full marks to them!—but there was no sign of the daughter in the photo! When this too was rejected as proof that she was being held, the kidnappers became peevish and childish. They insisted that a photograph be sent to them showing all the people over at her family's house holding different issues of a well-known sports magazine. They provided an address to send the photograph ... exactly what police needed to move in and make an arrest.

And as an explanatory footnote: The kooky kidnappers later admitted they did not understand the principle involved in the photograph/newspaper concept. 'We thought it was just some kind of tradition,' one said.

SOME HABITS DIE HARD

A convicted counterfeiter and bank robber negotiated a deal to pay $8500 in damages, rather than serve a prison sentence. For payment, he handed over a forged cheque. Ten years. Bang!

$16 + $16 = $?

Police arrested a young man at an airport hotel after he tried to pass two $16 bills. It was news to him when he discovered that the Mint doesn't actually print that particular denomination!

MONEY BAGS!

A robber was arrested after knocking out an armoured car driver and stealing four bags of money. Each bag contained $800 dollars in coins. The weight of the bags—about 10 kilograms each—slowed down our fleet-footed crim to a sluggish stagger. Police easily ran him down.

PLAY IT COOL, KIDS

A man and wife in their late twenties with two kids and lousy jobs were evicted from their house. So to solve their worries in one big bang, they decided to rob an armoured van. They planned the whole thing carefully, did the deed, and got away with $17 million. But instead of putting their illegally gained proceeds into a foreign account and sitting pretty for a while until the heat was off, they began to spend lavishly—a $2 million house, speedboats, a 'his' and 'hers' BMW ... Needless to say, since they both held minimum-wage jobs, this sudden excess of cash caught the eye of a number of authorities. They were investigated and caught ... duh!

EIGHT-TIME LOSER

A petrol station owner in a small town was having a quiet night until a driver pulled up just wanting to fill his tank. In a few swift moves, this amazing man proved that the simple things in life are really quite tricky—if you're completely blotto.

The owner sat and watched as the clearly inebriated man got out of the car and went through the motions of getting petrol. After a few misjudged aims at the fuel tank, he staggered towards the owner with a credit card in his hand. He dropped his card on the ground and fell over while asking if he could get some help with the pump. The owner went over with his drunk companion and watched as he proceeded to try and stick his credit card into every possible slot of the petrol pump. The owner assisted him to pay and then opened the door of his car—the entire driver's side was covered with vomit. The owner then asked him if he'd been drinking. The driver didn't answer but simply took out his mobile phone and a few seconds later handed it him, telling the service station owner that someone wanted to talk to him. He had called the police. Both men waited quietly for the police to arrive and the inebriated driver got into the police car without a struggle. As the police car pulled away, he wound down the window and explained to the petrol station owner that it was the eighth time he had been arrested that week.

A PICTURE'S WORTH A THOUSAND WORDS

An elderly woman was sitting in an instant photo booth at the airport getting her picture taken. A man stuck his head through the curtain and grabbed her handbag just as the camera flashed. As soon as the picture was developed, she took it to the police and the man was identified, caught, and arrested the next day. Snap!

INVISIBLE INFRA-RED

Two police officers responded to a call that several alarms were going off at a warehouse. When they got inside, they found that someone had placed cardboard boxes on top of all the motion detectors. They soon found the crook hiding in a corner and arrested him. But the thief was puzzled and wanted to know: 'How did you guys know I was here? I covered up all the security cameras so that you couldn't see me.'

FOOT FETISH

A guy broke into a woman's home and glued his foot to her face. No-one knows why because he's not saying. The couple then had to drive to the hospital to have the foot surgically removed. The guy was arrested after the surgery and was not allowed within 100 metres of any glue sticks ... only kidding!

CONCENTRATE!

A man walked into a convenience store with a shotgun under his coat. He pointed it at the cashier and demanded all the money she had, but then got distracted by the front cover of a magazine on display. He put his gun on the counter, walked over to the rack to browse, and then looked up to see the cashier pointing the gun at him.

UNDERCOOKED BRAIN CELLS?

Three men burst into a pizza shop one evening demanding cash and pizza. They got what they wanted and took off, but 20 minutes later they were back again ... to complain that their pizza was undercooked. As it happens, the police who responded to the robbery were pleased that they were saved the trouble of actually having to track them down!

SUSPICIOUS BEHAVIOUR

Why would a man inexplicably run from police when they spotted him loitering around a vending machine? That's what police wanted to know ... and they got their answer soon afterwards when the same guy tried to post his $400 bail entirely in coins.

ONLY KIDDING, OFFICERS

A man burst through the front doors and yelled, 'This is a hold-up!' His dramatic entrance didn't go down too well. Unfortunately, he had meant to rob the post office next door, but had picked the wrong entrance and found himself at the front desk of his local police station.

HEY, LET'S ROB A BANK

... and get caught!

Robbing a bank is what most criminals aspire to. It's the 'least effort for the greatest reward' scenario. Why work your guts out in a dead-end job when in five minutes flat you can have enough money to last you for the next 20 years? After all, there's nothing to it, is there? You just go in, get the money, and come out. Hmm. Strange as it may seem, so many things can go wrong when you rob a bank. You can get covered in exploding dye, you can get a flat tyre as you make your getaway, or you may come up against an unsympathetic teller who just refuses to hand over the money ... now that's really hard to take. But what most brain-cell deficient master criminals forget is this: you will get caught!

MR EXPERT GETS CAUGHT!

Police investigating a bank robbery of $8000 found the suspect sitting in his car two blocks away counting the money. What's more, he was certainly caught red-handed—some of the money included traceable bills known as 'bait bills'. Disappointingly, the criminal was a well-known author, radio host, and consultant on crime prevention who worked for some major insurance companies on detecting and avoiding crime. He even had qualifications in criminology! Police commented: 'For someone who is an expert on crime, he certainly made a lot of stupid mistakes.'

THAT REALLY BURNS ME UP!

A man wearing a large black and white sloppy joe gave a bank cashier a plastic shopping bag and demanded money. The cashier filled the bag with money and an explosive dye pack that burns at about

200?°C when activated. The man stuffed the bag down the front of his pants and ran from the bank. Witnesses then saw a wonderful sight, which they described as, 'an explosion taking place inside his trousers'. The bungling bandit began hopping and jumping around like a lunatic. The hot dye pack seared through the crotch of his trousers and burnt a hole through his fly. Screaming like a maniac and desperate for some relief, the robber stripped off his smouldering trousers and ran and ran and ran ... Police suspect he's sitting around with a packet of frozen peas in his lap. They have alerted local hospitals to be on the lookout for a man with green genitals who is complaining of crotch burns.

DARN, NO PAPER BAG!

A man walked into a bank and handed the teller a note, which read: 'Put all your money in a paper bag.' The teller wrote a note back saying: 'I don't have a paper bag.' The robber walked out, contemplating just how unfair life can be.

GREEDY GUTS!

A bank robber used two plastic garbage bags to haul the loot. He got so much money and the bags were so heavy that he had to drag them along the ground. He made it outside, but as he came down the front steps of the bank, one of the bags ripped open, spilling money all over the footpath. Police were happy to assist him with his little dilemma.

I WON THE LOTTERY ... REALLY!

A young man robbed a bank and made a clean getaway. He would never have been caught except for one small thing ... the next day he went back to the same bank to deposit the money into his account.

THANKS A LOT, DEAR!

A man returned to a town that he'd left when he separated from his wife. He had a definite purpose in mind—to rob a bank. He handed over a note demanding money, got some cash, and made a beeline for the door. He hightailed it out of town, figuring that no one would locate him at the scene of the crime.

As it happened, the only woman who could identify him was out and about that day. His ex-wife happened to be on her way to the same bank when she noticed his very distinctive truck—black with a chrome smokestack—rumbling out of town on the motorway. She got to wondering what he was doing in town.

Meanwhile, the man stopped at a creek bed, where he wrapped the money in a scarf and hid it under a rock until the coast was clear and he could return.

When our felon's ex-wife reached the bank, she discovered that it was closed. The gossip was that there had been a robbery. So she went to another branch with information that they were pleased to receive. She told management that she had seen her ex-husband in town shortly after the robbery and that he had just recently got out of prison after serving a sentence for bank robbery. The woman identified her ex from a photograph taken by the bank surveillance camera, and police took him into custody that afternoon. He did return to the creek but not alone—some nice police officers came along with him and were very interested in one particular rock.

SPEAK UP, I HAVE A GUN!

A man walked into a bank and demanded money. The teller asked, 'You want that in a bag?' The robber yelled back, 'You're darn right I have a gun!' Realising the robber was hard of hearing, the teller set off the alarm. Police arrived within minutes and arrested the partially deaf and very confused man.

WOE IS ME!

So many things can go wrong when you try to rob a bank—at least that's what one fellow found out when he raced out of a bank with a $3000 haul. As he attempted to leap into his getaway truck, the dye pack exploded, drenching him in bright red dye. Even more humiliating, he was arrested a short time later at a service station where he was madly trying to pump up his flat tyre.

THINK IT THROUGH, DUMBO!

This novice bank robber must win the prize for the stupidest series of mistakes. After handing the teller a handwritten note of demands, he grabbed the money and ran—so far, so good. Then our robber realised that he had better go back because he had forgotten the note, which would be used as incriminating evidence against him. He managed to grab the note and make his getaway for the second time. The problem was that when he reached his getaway car, he discovered that he had left the car keys at the bank. Wisely deciding to abandon the car, he made his way home with the money. Then he became just too clever for his own good. He had 'borrowed' his flatmate's car for the robbery (without telling her), so when she started worrying about the car, he told her that it must have been stolen. What did she do? She rang the police and reported her car stolen. Less than 20 minutes later, a police officer spotted the car right outside the bank. With the keys that had been left at the scene of the crime, the police officer tried to start the car and, hallelujah, they fitted! It's all too easy now. The police officer returned the car to the address the car owner had given him and arrested a highly embarrassed bank robber with a highly irate flatmate.

CURIOSITY KILLED THE CAT

A suspect wanted for questioning in relation to a bank robbery rang police to see if there were any other warrants out for his arrest. Needless to say, the answer was yes. Police showed up shortly after the phone call with three outstanding warrants and he was carted off to jail. Well, he did want to know!

NO CASH? I'LL TAKE A CHEQUE

An 18-year-old held up a man at gunpoint and demanded money. When the victim said he didn't have any money, our ski-masked friend told him to write him a cheque—which he did. Unbeknownst to the robber, it's quite easy to stop payment on a cheque—which the victim did. And so the next day, the robber was arrested as he attempted to cash it. Police investigating the case said they'd never heard of an armed robbery that involved writing a cheque!

LUCKY BREAK!

Two police detectives couldn't believe their luck when they were walking past a bank one afternoon and saw a man they were very keen to speak to. He was standing in line to see a teller and fitted the description of a suspect wanted for a series of bank heists. They watched the man for a while before entering the bank to get a closer look. Unseen, they managed to stand right behind him and overhear his conversation with the teller. Weren't they amazed when, right in front of their eyes, he pulled out a gun and attempted to rob the bank! The man was equally amazed to be arrested instantly ... police these days are sure quick at the scene.

WHO WAS THAT MASKED MAN?

Criminals who can't resist making a fashion statement

More than 75 per cent of criminals don't bother to wear a disguise. That's the thing about dumb crooks, they think they are infallible, impervious to gunshot wounds, and unrecognisable in broad daylight. Then there are the small-time crims who wear masks so silly that their intended victims just look at them in disbelief and laugh in their face. And that's certainly not what an edgy, inexperienced crook needs. At the other extreme are the crooks who are so organised that they put on their disguises way too early. Like the guy who got to his first bank heist before opening time, so he put his complete bandit costume on and waited patiently in line with the other customers, not realising that he stood out like a sore thumb. But slipping into disguise way too early is better than way too late, right? Like the guy who rushed in, pulled out his pistol, made some threats ... and then fumbled around trying to adjust the mask he had forgotten to put on. You really have to wonder ...

ESKY HEAD

A would-be thief entered a convenience store, grabbed a foam esky, punched a hole in it so he could see, and put it over his head. Then he went up to the assistant and demanded money. Problem was, she couldn't understand a word he was saying.

THE BUTT OF THE JOKE?

A 43-year-old man dropped in at a convenience store where he showed off his 'porno pants'—a pair of jeans with the backside cut out, except for a thin strip of material down the middle. But the folks in the store weren't amused and called the police. The man told officers he had been stripping at a private party nearby and was still in a festive mood, so he thought it would be fun to stop by at a local store to see how people would react. They reacted by arresting him for lewd behaviour.

FACE IN THE CROWD

A man wearing pantyhose on his face carried out a daring daylight raid in a crowded shopping centre. The shop assistant rang for security and two guards rushed towards the scene. When he saw them coming, the thief grabbed a shopping bag, slowed down to a sauntering pace, and pretended to be window-shopping. The only trouble was, he forgot to take the pantyhose off his head!

PEEK A BOO!

A service station attendant had no trouble identifying a robber for police, even though the man had worn a pair of women's panties over his head as a brilliant disguise. The thief admitted that his judgment wasn't that great due to the amount of alcohol he had consumed. The panties as a disguise could have worked, except that he stuck his face through one of the leg-holes so he could see.

NO, REALLY, I CAN'T BREATHE!

A man wearing a pair of pantyhose on his head as a disguise was midway through holding up a bank. Then before the anxious teller's eyes, he started coughing and gasping for breath. She wasn't sure if he was kidding around or not until he collapsed to the ground and didn't move any more. He had to be rushed to hospital—he was about to suffocate!

THIS SUIT IS KILLING ME!

Some people like dressing up in seventies disco gear; some people like impersonating police officers. Well, this particular gent loved dressing up as a veritable knight of the Round Table in a full suit of armour.

One night, fully clad as Sir Lancelot, he decided to rob a house a few doors down, but he forgot to take into account the fact that a suit of armour makes a fair amount of noise. The clanging metal made such a din that the owners of the home heard him as soon as he busted through the door. They pushed a bookcase on top of the would-be knight, which was a good move, because it damaged his armour so badly that he couldn't get up ... and he couldn't get out of his suit. The force of the bookcase had welded it to his body! At his hearing, heads turned as he took to the stand still wearing the dented suit of armour. It was suggested that a locksmith be found to put him out of his misery.

CARL OR CARLA?

A man snatched a woman's bag as she was walking down the street. After finding a pay cheque in her purse, he tried to cash it ... by dressing in drag! It might have turned out okay for him, except that the teller noticed that the cheque was made out to her daughter.

COVERED WITH NACHO CHEESE

A police officer on late shift stopped to investigate a jeep parked at a swimming pool complex at 5.00 a.m. one Sunday morning. He saw an open bottle of vodka in the console along with various articles of clothing, so he stuck around to see whether the owner would be coming back.

Minutes later, he couldn't believe his eyes when a nude man—smeared with nacho cheese—dashed out of the pool complex and ran towards the jeep. This interesting figure smelled strongly of alcohol and had nacho cheese coating his hair, face and shoulders. He was also carrying a cardboard box. The officer had a word with him and confiscated the cardboard box. Inside were $40 worth of chips and corn chips. Apparently, our cheesy streaker had scaled the three-metre fence, broken into the snack bar, and scattered cheese and chips all over the ground. And all this he carried out completely starkers and covered in cheese. The 21-year-old celebrated his birthday in custody and was charged with burglary, theft, vandalism, and public intoxication. Was it really worth it for $40 worth of snacks?

PUNCTUALITY PLUS!

Some criminals behave just like fine upstanding citizens. Take a certain fellow who didn't want to be late for his first bank job. Knowing the bank opened at 10.00 a.m., he arrived at 9.45 and waited outside politely in line with the other customers—only thing was, he was dressed in full robbery gear: hooded sweater, gloves and face mask. As a police officer later observed: 'You have to wonder what they're thinking' or, *if* they are thinking.

QUICK-CHANGE ARTIST

Much to his surprise, a bank robber was caught very quickly after his first heist, even though he was wearing completely different clothing to what he had worn at the bank. His plan was to slip into jogging gear and jog off through the park and make his getaway. But for some bizarre reason, he stripped off and did his quick change right outside the bank, in full view of the customers and tellers, who were able to tell the police precisely what he looked like and what he was wearing.

HE LOVES PLAYING DRESS-UPS!

A police officer was driving to his late shift at about 10.30 p.m. one night when he saw a red car ahead of him pull up on the top of a hill. As the officer drove past the stopped car, the driver shone a spotlight in his face. The car then pulled in behind the officer's vehicle and the driver activated a flashing blue light on the dashboard.

The police officer didn't pull over for two reasons: one, there were no police markings on the car; and two, the law in this particular state requires police vehicles to use red lights, not blue ones. So, thinking something was up, the officer slowed down to get the licence plate number of the car behind him, but as he did so, the red car slowed down too and didn't overtake him.

Since he was on his way to work and officially 'off duty', the officer called dispatchers on his mobile and another car responded to the call. As the police vehicle approached, the red car sped away and led the two police officers on a merry chase. Officers placed spikes on the roadway and flattened three tyres until finally their suspect lost control and crashed into a telegraph pole. He scrambled out, unhurt, and leapt over several backyard fences before making his way back home. There police found a gold badge, a police scanner, a list of police radio frequencies, a night stick, handcuffs, and other police paraphernalia. It appeared that the red car driver was an out-of-work security guard who just liked pretending to be a police officer. But it was a bit of bad luck that out of all the people to try and pull over, he picked a police officer on his way to work.

ELVIS HAS LEFT THE BUILDING

A man walked into a restaurant one morning and went straight to the men's bathroom. He emerged 10 minutes later in full Elvis regalia— dark blue jumpsuit, dark glasses, a not-very-authentic Elvis mask, BUT no blue suede shoes. He approached the cashier and held out a bag, demanding money with his hand in his pocket as if he had a weapon. When the cashier didn't react immediately and hand over the money, he got irritated and went out the back.

Elvis was last seen exiting the building. Unfortunately for him, witnesses who saw the man before he put on his mask, all agreed that he had quite severe acne scars on his face. So our poor old rocker was quite easy to identify.

GOOD DISGUISE

A tall, well-dressed man with a briefcase walked into a bank. He stood in line just as any other customer would. As he got closer to the teller, he opened his briefcase and pulled out a ski mask and a gun. He then calmly continued to wait in line. Strangely, he never did get his chance to rob the bank.

BAD IDEA, BALDY!

A man went into a liquor store, pointed a gun at the woman behind the counter, and demanded money. Good plan, but there was only one problem—a security guard just happened to be watching the video from the store's surveillance camera and got a good look at the robber's face. The security guard then tracked the man as he left the store, assuming he would return home. But he didn't. He went into the rest room at a nearby petrol station. Ten minutes later he came out. He was still carrying the stolen cash and his gun, but he had a bold new look—he had completely shaved his head in a classic disguise attempt! Unfortunately he didn't fool the two men waiting for him— the security guard and his backup.

ABSOLUTE BEGINNER

A robber burst into a bank with a hessian bag over his head. Good disguise, except that he forgot to cut out any eyeholes. Bumping into customers on his way to the teller, he then pulled out his weapons of assault—a plastic knife and a toy pistol. Needing some fresh air, he then lifted the front of his mask to demand money and the security camera got a good full-frontal shot of him. You'd think that after all the trouble he went to that he'd get the dough. But no, the teller told our well-prepared friend that she couldn't open the safe. At this point, he gave up and ran away.

TAKE YOUR HAT OFF, BUD

On his way home from work, a construction worker decided to rob a shop. Problem was he wore his hard hat, which had his name and the name of his construction company in BIG BLACK LETTERS!

HAVEN'T YOU FORGOTTEN SOMETHING?

What NOT to do when committing a crime

Some people thrive under pressure and are at their best when confronted with complex new situations; other people crack under stress. The first group is ideally suited to a life of crime; the second should definitely pursue some other career path. It's surprising how many thieves lose their nerve and make really stupid mistakes, no matter how experienced they are. They leave their ID at the scene of the crime, they smile for the security cameras, or they leave a bank with less money than they started out with! The following stories all have something in common. Each and every crook needs a friendly guardian angel to be with them as they attempt their crime, and to whisper in their ear as they are about to make their escape: 'Haven't you forgotten something?'

LOVE THY NEIGHBOUR?

A woman taking a nap was woken by the sound of her back door slamming. She jumped up and ran downstairs to find the door open and her VCR missing from the top of her TV.

The woman next door had a drug habit and the victim's suspicions were aroused when she found some keys on the kitchen table that didn't belong to her. When police knocked on her neighbour's door there was no answer, so they tried the keys—perfect fit!

USE WRAPPING PAPER NEXT TIME

A police unit was trying to uncover the identity of a major drug dealer. The unit had made several controlled drug purchases but couldn't find out much about the dealer except that he seemed to own a restaurant in the city. Things began to look promising when they were able to arrange a face-to-face drop, but the tailing team lost him. In the next transaction, the police couldn't believe it—the drugs were wrapped in a takeaway menu, which they assumed was from the restaurant the dealer owned. But they struck gold on the next deal— the drugs were folded up in the dealer's mobile phone bill!

TUG OF WAR

Two men tried to pull the front panel off an ATM by running a chain from the machine to the bumper of their pick-up truck. Instead of pulling the front of the machine off, they pulled off their front bumper bar. They panicked and fled, leaving the chain, bumper bar, and numberplate all beautifully arranged for police to follow up.

BIRDBRAIN BOMBER?

One evening, a police officer went to respond to a homeowner's request for assistance. It appeared that someone had attempted to blow up his mailbox by putting a suspicious-looking device inside. The homeowner was totally on edge because he didn't know whether the bomb was set to go off or not. When the officer arrived and took a look inside the mailbox, sure enough, he saw a small bottle wrapped in black electrical tape. There was some black powder inside too.

The officer took the 'bomb' back to headquarters where, on closer inspection, it was found that the bottle was a common medicine phial. The officer decided to cut the black tape away and what did he find? The pharmacy label printed with the would-be bomber's name and address as clear as day.

HAVEN'T YOU
FORGOTTEN SOMETHING?

Two inexperienced bank robbers went into a bank and told the cashier they wanted to open new accounts. The cashier asked for their ID. They obliged by handing over their driver's licences. Then one of them pulled out a pistol and demanded cash. The cashier got $50 000 from the safe and handed it over to the men who then scooted. You can guess what happened. They had left their IDs behind ... but in their hurry to get out the door they also forgot to take the cash!

DON'T FORGET TO SAY THANK YOU

A man walked into a convenience store and demanded all the money. He said thank you very politely, turned, and walked out, forgetting the money. Realising his oversight, he went back and was arrested.

HIRE-AN-IDIOT

Police didn't have to look very hard for clues in the robbery of a local credit union. The suspects left behind a car rental receipt, which noted that the car had to be returned that evening. So, police waited patiently for the suspects to bring the car back. And they hadn't even thought to get rid of the evidence—police found the cash and a pellet gun inside the vehicle.

WALLET, MOBILE AND FINGERPRINTS ... YOU'VE WON THE TRIFECTA!

In a ploy to get a liquor store owner to open the till, a robber took his wallet out to pay for a can of beer. But in the confusion, as three other members of the gang ransacked the shop and they all fled, he forgot he had left the wallet on the counter. Adding to his impressive bungling, he dropped his mobile phone, which had his number in the memory, and he didn't wear gloves so his fingerprints were all over the beer can. Well done, mate!

CHECK THE FUEL GAUGE

A driver pulled into a service station late one night with an empty petrol tank, but the service station was closed. While he was figuring out what to do, a car-jacker ran up and took the car at gunpoint. The victim told him that the car was out of petrol but the adrenalin-charged car-jacker jumped in anyway. The victim immediately rang the police and watched as the car went putt-putting down the street until it stalled about 100 metres from where it started.

X-RAY EYES

A forgetful thief broke into an elderly woman's house and stole her life savings, valued at almost $43 000 in cash. When police came to investigate, the woman told them she had found something that didn't belong to her and she handed them a large manila envelope. Inside was a set of X-rays for a broken arm, complete with the patient's name, phone number and address.

Police were pleased that the 'anonymous' intruder had left his calling card—it made their job that much easier. Standing at his front door, with his left arm clearly in a plaster cast, he denied all until presented with the X-rays. Then he confessed that he had done the break-in on the way home from hospital, as you do!

DARLING, ABOUT THAT LINGERIE ...

Late one night after a heavy drinking session, a usually mild-mannered man came up with a wild and crazy scheme. Wearing a pair of underpants on his head, he carried out a brazen but surprisingly successful robbery. The next morning he had no recollection of where he had been the night before, so he was rather surprised to find a large unexplained wad of cash in his pocket. As the pieces of the puzzle started falling into place, his suspicions were confirmed when he saw a photograph of the hold-up in the paper. The masked man was wearing a familiar pair of knickers over his head—they belonged to his wife!

HERE, TAKE MY MONEY!

A man walked into a convenience store, put a $20 note on the counter, and asked for change. When the shop assistant opened the register, the man pulled out a gun and told her to give him all the money. She did. The man grabbed the money and fled, leaving his original $20 behind. His total haul—$15 minus the $20 he left behind. Which raises an interesting question: if someone points a gun at you and gives you money, is that a stick-up?

MASTER OF DISGUISE

A robber with a true genius for disguise was recorded at two robberies. In the first, he was captured on the store's closed circuit surveillance camera outside the store, practising pulling his shirt up to be used as a mask. In the second, his target was a motel a block away from the store and he was again captured practising his disguise. In that robbery, his 'mask' was a towel with two eyeholes cut out of it. Seems the suspect entered the motel, pointed the gun at the clerk and demanded money. Then he realised he'd forgotten to put his 'mask' on, so he tried—very surreptitiously—to put on the mask and line up the eyeholes with his eyes while committing the robbery. It didn't work.

BAD TIMING, BOYS

Bank staff were holding their weekly meeting just before opening on Monday morning. That's when they witnessed two men wearing ski masks rush up to the front doors and try to get in. Problem was the doors were still locked. After pushing, pulling, bashing and head-butting the glass doors, the pair realised they were locked. Shaken by the experience, they ran off, forgetting that their getaway car was parked right outside.

STEP OUTSIDE!

A man with a fear of flying was trying to conquer his fear by going on a short flight. Before he boarded the plane, he unwisely thought he would calm his nerves by drinking a whole bottle of vodka. Once on board, he was fairly tetchy and it wasn't long before he got into an argument with another passenger. As things spiralled out of control, our vodka-fuelled fool challenged the other man to 'step outside and say that'. He kind of forgot he was flying 8000 metres above sea level. Much to his good fortune, flight attendants were able to subdue him before he made it to the door to carry out his threat. And what does he face apart from an even greater fear of flying? Disorderly conduct charges.

BLING BLING RING!

A noticeably cool dude wearing lots of jewellery and the latest streetwear, came into a motel and inquired about a room. He came back a short time later, took out a pistol and demanded money. He then tied up the receptionist and jumped the counter. That's when things started to go wrong. He tried to remove the hotel safe, but it was bolted to the floor and wouldn't budge, so he tried to open it where it was, but he couldn't. As he scurried about looking for another source of money, he realised there was a video camera filming everything. So he grabbed the VCR near the camera and fled.

Poor guy. He took the wrong VCR, because the one that was connected to the security camera was actually in a locked office. Naturally, police were able to get a good description of the man, especially since he stopped twice to preen himself in front of the camera. And they didn't have to bother with an extensive search ... he returned to reception later that afternoon to try and retrieve a $2500 ring that he'd lost during the hold-up.

LEAVE THE MONEY AND RUN?

A first-time bank robber gave six $50 bills to a teller and asked her to exchange them for hundreds. As she did, the man pulled a ski mask over his face and put his hand in his pocket, pretending he had a gun. When the teller looked up and saw the masked man, she screamed and ducked down behind the counter. The robber lost his nerve and ran out of the bank, leaving behind his $300.

MUG SHOTS FOR BIG MUGS!

Three boys broke into a school and went on a rampage, breaking windows and emptying desk drawers. When they got bored with their mindless vandalism, they started playing with the photocopier, taking prints of their backsides and their faces. Next morning police went through the screwed up pieces of paper on the floor and found perfect mug shots of each of the boys involved.

FAIR ENOUGH

A man walked into a liquor store, pulled out a gun and said, 'Give me everything in the register'. The clerk told him there was no money in the register. The would-be robber scooted, explaining amiably, 'That's okay, there are no bullets in the gun!'

CAMERA CAPERS

Three mates noticed a young woman taking pictures with a high-tech camera, so they wandered over and one of them grabbed it right out of her hands. Bad idea. She was an undercover cop doing surveillance work and backup officers immediately swarmed onto the scene, grabbing one of the men before he had a chance to scoot. The second of the trio managed to get away, thoughtfully dropping a nice range of incriminating evidence along the way including a gun, some drugs, and other stolen items. After the cops pinned him down, they turned their attention to dumb crook number three. He had the brains to jump into his truck and zoom out of there, but he was blocked off by highway patrol cars within a couple of kilometres. With no escape route open, he clambered out of the vehicle and tried to run. Sadly, he forgot to put the truck into 'park' and it ran over him. Although, happily as it turns out, he was eventually well enough to join the other two in jail.

FLASHER WITH CREDIT

Two women were minding their own business, doing some grocery shopping, when a 23-year-old man started following them. He then sashayed past them with his penis exposed and gave them a wink.

Security located the suspect on videotape and were able to follow his path through the store, where they determined he had made a purchase at a front checkout counter. Unluckily for him, the flasher had used his credit card so police were able to track him down.

ANONYMOUS?

You'd think people working in technology would be able to use their brains, but sometimes it just doesn't work that way. A supposedly smart bunch of employees of a large aerospace company came up with a foolproof idea—they would rob a bank during their lunch hour. They felt sure they would easily get away with the plan and the best part is that the police would never think of looking for them at the plant. One small detail lead to their downfall—they forgot to take their ID badges off during the robbery.

IT'S SMART TO CHECK REFERENCES!

A gang of bank robbers who had worked together for two very lucrative years planned a new series of robberies. At the last minute, one of them broke his leg so they had to hire a new bloke to drive the getaway car. The first break-in was a great success; laden with several bags of loot, the robbers rushed out of the bank towards the waiting car. The new driver panicked and the car stalled. He was still trying to get the car to start when the police arrived. In court, it was revealed that not only did the man not have a driver's licence, he had never driven a car before.

TROUSERS DOWN, GENTLEMEN

A flasher exposed himself to a woman in a park, but didn't notice there was a police car nearby. When she yelled out, police approached and the man took off. He didn't get very far. He tripped over his own trousers, which he'd forgotten to zip up before running away.

CHECK THE OIL TOO!

A man suspected of three bank robberies tried for a fourth, but wasn't so lucky. He walked into the bank and gave the teller a piece of paper. The note said that there was a car full of explosives outside and he would set it off if they didn't comply with his request. The teller handed him an undisclosed amount of money and he fled.

A witness told police that he had driven off in a silver Mazda. She also noticed that one of the car's tyres appeared to be nearly flat.

Police began checking auto shops in the area and found their suspect at a nearby garage buying a much-needed new tyre with proceeds from his robbery.

HEY, IT'S DARK IN HERE!

A newsagency was the scene of a very entertaining attempted robbery. Two teenagers entered the shop and proclaimed: 'This is a stick-up!' The first oversight they made was that they forgot to bring the gun and as soon as they realised this, they started bickering with each other about whose fault it was. But their biggest faux pas was really impressive ... they forgot to cut eyeholes in their masks.

Customers watched in astonishment as the pair re-enacted a Three Stooges comedy, repeatedly bumping into each other, and demanding money from the shop wall instead of the shop owner. Of course, not being able to see, they failed to notice the owner telephoning the police.

The grand finale was when they crashed into the shop counter and ripped off their masks in frustration—right in front of the security camera.

TWO FOR THE PRICE OF ONE?

A young man forced a commuter at a train station to hand over his wallet. After taking the cash, he meant to hand the empty wallet back to the victim, but in the heat of the moment, he got mixed up ... and handed back his own wallet.

NUDIE BEER!

A burglar really made himself at home one night. He found a cold beer in the fridge, stripped off, and had a relaxing evening lying in bed watching TV. But when the homeowners returned unexpectedly just before midnight, he jumped up and sprinted out the front door. We can conclude that this robber wasn't that brilliant. Firstly he didn't actually steal anything (except a beer). And secondly, in his haste to escape without being identified, he left his shorts, singlet, wallet and ID on the bed.

HAPPY SNAPS

Two men went into a photo shop to pick up some holiday snaps and while they were there decided to steal an expensive digital camera. While one distracted the salesperson, the other pocketed the camera. They then ran off, leaving their photographs behind.

BEEN WATCHING TOO MANY MOVIES?

Industrial thieves broke into a chemical plant by crossing a metal catwalk, and then blew it up, having forgotten that it was their only means of escape.

JUST BORROWING THE CAR

It's not unheard of for someone to go for a test drive in a new car and never come back. That's what one man did with a specific purpose in mind—he used the stolen vehicle as a getaway car in a bank robbery. Obligingly, he left a copy of his driver's licence at the car dealer's and, even more obligingly, he got a mate to return the car for him the next day. Police set up surveillance at the suspect's apartment and arrested him as he left for work in a new car—a car that he'd bought (not stolen!) after the bank robbery.

A STORY WITH BITE

Late one evening, a man broke into a vacant house that was being renovated. The next morning, the owner found an odd baseball cap on the garage floor and called police. Nothing seemed to have been stolen, so after making their report, police left the scene. But about four hours later, the owner's aunt was double checking for missing things in the garage when she came upon an interesting discovery— a pair of false teeth lying on the floor! Investigators suspect that the robber tripped on something in the garage and lost his dentures as well as his baseball cap.

After calling several dentists' offices, police learned that the dentures had the owner's name on them, hidden underneath the fake gum, as required by state law. The dental assistant who helped police with inquiries was thrilled to be involved: 'It was a unique experience to get that call from the police. In all the time I have worked here, no-one has ever called about lost dentures!'

When police arrived at the suspect's house, he didn't have any teeth. They returned them to him so he could confess to the crime on tape and then allowed him to have his teeth back for good after he signed it for them. 'It was a first for me,' said the investigating officer. 'I have never caught someone with their teeth before.'

PRETTY POLLY TELL POLICE?

A bird only narrowly missed being kidnapped because of its big mouth. Three men ransacked a house but were alarmed when the family's parrot began repeating the nickname of one of the men. They made their exit, then had second thoughts and rushed back inside to snatch their feathered informant. Unfortunately for the bird-brained trio, their timing was out and as they made their exit for the second time, the police made their entrance.

IDENTITY CRISIS

*Criminals who pretend to be
someone else or forget who they are!*

Being a dumb crook requires no special training, but it does help if you are slow-witted, a hopeless liar, and very forgetful. For some of these fearless fools, it's hard enough to remember their own name, let alone get an alibi right. Some crooks come up with interesting ways to avoid admitting who they really are. They decide to run their own little law enforcement crusades and impersonate traffic cops just for the heck of it. Others get confused about who they're out to get and hone in on the wrong victim, often with hilarious results. And then there are those who give police a false name, and then forget just what the name was. Believe me, a crook having an identity crisis is a very confused person!

DO THEY DRIVE BMWS UP THERE?

A well-dressed middle-aged man was stopped for speeding and the police officer asked to see his driver's licence. The man dug into the glove box and willingly handed his papers over. His car registration and driver's licence were in the name of 'Saint Peter', issued by 'the Kingdom of Heaven'.

WHO AM I AGAIN?

Police had information about the whereabouts of a woman wanted on three charges of felony. On gaining entrance to the suspect's house, police did a search but could not find her. There was one door that hadn't been checked—a door off the master bedroom. So, after announcing his intentions, an officer flung open the door ... and there was the woman in question. Following standard procedure, they asked her what her name was and she said, 'Alison'. Then they asked her husband her name and he declared it was 'Beth'. The first officer made yet another attempt. He told her to stand up as she was under arrest and asked her again what her name was. This time it was 'Caroline'. Police guess that they had scared her so badly that she couldn't even remember her false name.

SHOULDN'T YOU BE INSIDE?

Police spent two hours attempting to subdue a gunman who had barricaded himself inside his own home. After firing 10 tear gas canisters, officers discovered that the man was standing beside them, shouting pleas to come out and give himself up.

LET'S PRETEND I'M A BANK ROBBER!

A man pretending to have a gun kidnapped a motorist and forced him to drive to two different ATMs. The kidnapper then proceeded to withdraw money from his own bank accounts.

THE NEW EMPLOYEE

A man walked into an instant print shop and demanded all their money. Apparently, he wasn't satisfied with the haul, so in an ingenious move, he tied up the woman behind the counter and took her place. Smilingly, he dealt with (and duped) customers himself for the next three hours until police showed up and nabbed him.

I'M NOT STAN AND I'M NOT IN

A woman contacted police after she began receiving prank phone calls one day. A police officer went to her house and as he was getting the details, the phone rang. The woman answered on one extension and the police officer listened on another. As he listened the officer realised that he recognised the caller's voice. He spoke to the caller loudly and distinctly saying only his name. The caller responded with an amazed 'What!' The officer told him who he was and that he would be coming to his home shortly and then he hung up. But unbelievably, within a couple of minutes, the phone rang again. Once again the woman and the officer both picked up the phone. It was the same caller asking the woman if he could speak with the police officer.

'What do you want, Stan?' said the officer.

'This isn't Stan,' he replied.

'Well, I'll be coming over to your place very soon.'

'I'm not at home,' said Stan. 'I'm at Bob's house!'

IT'S ONLY TV!

During the filming of the weekly TV series *Homicide,* production was interrupted when two criminals, fleeing the scene of their crime, surrendered to a bunch of actors dressed up like police. The bad guys thought that they had been 'headed off' by the real cops!

I'M ALL ALONE ...
EXCEPT FOR THIS NAKED MAN!

Four police raided an apartment early one morning after being tipped-off that a suspect was living there with his girlfriend. They got into position and one of them knocked loudly on the door. From the bedroom window, a man's voice was clearly heard swearing loudly and then asking who the hell was waking him up at this time of the morning. The answer came back: 'Parole officers!'

Suddenly silence. After knocking twice more, a woman answered the door wearing only a nightshirt. Officers asked if the man of the house was at home. She said that she was alone and no-one was with her.

After searching the house, officers found the suspect hiding in her closet, completely naked. The woman feigned surprise. 'That's not the man you want,' she said. 'That's my brother!'

IT'S NOT ROCKET SCIENCE

Police were dealing with a case involving obscene phone calls. Although they had a suspect and knew the number of the mobile phone that the calls were coming from, they didn't have sufficient evidence to connect the phone to the suspect, but they were hot on his trail. So, one of the officers went to the suspect's home and spoke to him about it. He, of course, indignantly denied owning the phone or making any such calls. So the police officer took matters into his own hands. He got out his mobile phone and dialled the number that the obscene calls were coming from. Right in front of his eyes, the suspect brought out a ringing mobile phone from his pocket and answered it—sprung!

FUN AT THE FAIR

An 18-year-old lady went up to the ticket booth at a country fair and told them that her 12-year-old sister was lost inside. After filling out a missing persons report, sympathetic authorities allowed her to enter the fairground to look for her sister. Meanwhile, dozens of reserve deputies were called in to conduct their own search.

Authorities didn't get suspicious until the fair closed at midnight and they had not heard a peep from the young lady. Something didn't sound right because, although investigators were called in, there was no sign of her and despite repeated attempts, she was unable to be contacted.

Eventually, officers contacted the young woman's parents who told them what they had begun to suspect—that there was no 12-year-old sister. The whole thing was contrived to get into the fair for free.

Just a harmless prank? Hardly. A considerable number of officials had wasted a lot of time looking for a non-existent missing person. The young lady was charged with resisting, obstructing or delaying the duties of a public officer, and falsely reporting an emergency.

I AM NOT A SEX OFFENDER!

A man, let's call him Sam Dumble, had four drink driving arrests which he believed would make it difficult for him to get a driver's licence legally. So he stole the name and identity of his next door neighbour whom we shall call Brian Nasty. Everything went well until Dumble was arrested for disorderly conduct. A routine computer check found that 'Brian Nasty' was a convicted sex offender who was not registered as required. Dumble was adamant that he was not a convicted sex offender, but every bit of identification in his possession labelled him as 'Brian Nasty'. Finally, a check of his fingerprints revealed that the man purporting to be 'Brian Nasty' was in reality, Sam Dumble. Phew! At least the police recognised that he wasn't a sex offender, but he still got booked for criminal impersonation, identity theft, and forgery. A good rule of thumb for an identity thief: do not steal the name of someone whose reputation is worse than yours.

AM I A POLICE OFFICER OR A CROOK?

A 36-year-old police officer was charged with armed robbery. He confessed that he had robbed a bank and later investigated the crime himself, telling reporters at the time that police had no clues.

An hour after the crime, the police officer had returned to the bank as a leading investigator handling the case. Colleagues became suspicious when he bought a new car a month after the incident, paying in cash. Even more suspicious was the fact that the notes were traced ... and they were the banknotes stolen during the robbery.

HERE, HAVE MY LICENCE!

Two patrol officers were showing off the computer in their police car to kids at a school fun day. A young guy came up and asked how the system worked. The police asked for some ID to use for the demo. The man gave them his driver's licence. They entered it into the computer and moments later arrested him—the information that came up on the screen showed that he was wanted for an armed robbery two years earlier!

OFFICER WHO?

A 22-year-old man found an entertaining way to wile away those idle moments—he impersonated a police officer and got a buzz out of pulling motorists over and giving them mini-lectures about their driving. It appeared that he had been posing as a police officer for about two years before he was found out. His downfall came when he actually called in for assistance when one of his victims fled. Our delusional cop told investigators he had been working as a 'volunteer deputy' for about two years and that traffic violations were his 'thing'.

So, authorities investigating the case set to work to determine how extensive his masquerade was. They circulated a photograph of the man and received an overwhelming number of calls by motorists who had been pulled over by the phoney cop. Seems he was pretty busy doing his civic duties. They estimate that he had pulled over more than 200 motorists in just over a year—and that's just the ones they knew about. 'We've never seen anything to this extent,' said a police spokesperson. 'It's one thing to pretend you're a police officer, but when you call for backup you're just asking to get caught.'

MAMA, IT'S YOUR SON!

Two home invaders broke into a man's home, bound him with wire, and then robbed him, stealing $2500 cash, $5000 worth of jewellery, and a CD player. One of the home invaders also stole the man's bank account.

The next morning, the home invader tried to make a withdrawal from the man's account. The only problem was, the victim's mother was the bank's branch manager. When she was told by the tellers that a man identifying himself as her son was trying to make a withdrawal, she challenged his identity. He insisted strenuously that he was indeed her son; she challenged him again, and so it went on until he got restless and tried to get away from this woman who was hassling him. By then police had been informed and our villain didn't make it out the door.

JUST OUT FOR A RIDE ... AT 4.00 A.M.!

A couple were awakened at 4.00 a.m. one morning when someone lobbed a firebomb into their backyard. The Molotov cocktail—a petrol-filled wine bottle with sparklers strapped to it—failed to ignite but landed right next to their dog's kennel and set him off, barking madly.

When the homeowner—who was a former police officer—raced outside to see what was happening, he saw an elderly man standing there with his moped. The elderly man told him that he had nothing to do with the firebomb. He had just gone for a ride and happened to stop there because he had noticed his moped light wasn't working. But the homeowner wasn't convinced. So police were called and managed to untangle the real story. Apparently our elderly daredevil had an on-going five-year feud with a man he claimed had stolen his $1 million winning lottery ticket. All he had wanted to do was threaten his nemesis. The trouble is that he had the wrong house ... the man he was out to get had moved house a couple of months earlier.

THE NAME'S EXPRESS, SPEED EXPRESS

Desperate people try to cash some very suspicious-looking cheques, but this story wins the award for sheer nerve. A sharply dressed 18-year-old walked up to a bank teller with a $715.47 cheque that he wanted to cash. It was made out to a trucking company called Speed Express. Fine so far. The teller asked the man whether he was the owner of the company.

'No,' he said. 'My first name is Speed and my last name is Express.'

To prove it, the customer took out a fake photo ID and, sure enough, there was his name: Mr Speed Express. Oddly enough, the teller was still just a wee bit sceptical about the true identity of his new client, Mr Express. So he went away and put through a call to the trucking company. He spoke to a supervisor there who told him that the cheque had been stolen. Our canny teller then returned to his uniquely named customer and happily discussed fees with him and chatted with him until the police arrived to transport Mr Express away.

DEAD FUNNY

A shocked bank customer found it hard to put into words what she witnessed one morning as she waited in line at the bank. Three people, believed to be loan sharks, pushed a corpse in a wheelchair into the branch to make a pension withdrawal!

The woman says she saw three people pull up outside the bank, unload a wheelchair, and then struggle to force a lifeless body into the chair. They then wheeled their 'cousin' inside the bank and proceeded straight to the teller. When the teller requested that the dead body sign, the man said he was sick and that he was his next of kin. But the teller insisted that they wake Mr Dead-As-A-Doornail. The ruse was up when another bank teller became suspicious and attempted to check the wheelchair-bound man's pulse. Police were called in to discuss the matter with the fraudsters. Three of the four involved were happy to respond to questioning; the fourth one just sat there with a glazed expression on his face.

MY NAME IS ... ER, HANG ON!

A guy with an outstanding warrant—whom we shall refer to as 'Eric Moroney'—was seen at a bar and three police officers responded to the call. They found the fellow in the car park about to leave. One of the officers immediately confirmed that he was indeed the guy they were looking for and started to handcuff him. But good old Eric insisted that his name was Will Champion. He had never heard of this Eric person and surely they were mistaken. A second police officer came over and also personally recognised Eric from a string of earlier offences. But Eric valiantly continued to insist that he was, in fact, Will Champion. Finally, the third officer asked Eric to spell out his last name. Eric looked up at the night sky and began: M-O-R-O-N ... He instantly let out a loud groan and slapped his forehead with his hand. So much for an alias; he'd spelt his own name!

PROOF OF IDENTITY

A secretary was at work in a small country town when a friendly young man came in. He explained that he had a flat tyre and asked if she had a jack. When she told him she didn't, he asked to use her phone. She said that would be fine, but he never did make that call. As he reached for the phone, he noticed a photocopier. He explained that he was about to go for a job interview and wondered if she would mind making a copy of his birth certificate for the interview. She was happy to oblige since he was such a pleasant young man. She copied the front of the certificate and showed it to him. When she turned around to make a copy of the other side, she heard her car keys jingle behind her. She turned around in time to see him sprint out of the office with her purse and car keys. Then she looked down and shook her head in amazement ... she had his original birth certificate in her hand. The police, naturally, were grateful for the clue. As far as evidence goes, that's about the best you can get.

CAN I BE OF ASHISHTANCE, OFFISHER?

A man who stopped to offer assistance to a police officer on the side of the road ended up being charged with drink driving and losing his licence when he inadvertently ran into the back of the police officer's car. Furthermore, when asked for ID, he handed over his passenger's licence to save his own neck. His passenger happened to have an outstanding warrant for his arrest. It was not a good night for either of them.

TRAILS OF DESTRUCTION

Criminals who leave those little tell-tale signs!

The idea of pulling off the perfect crime is that no-one knows you've done it. Get the idea? You're able to sneak home, put your feet up, and count your loot with no fear of any pesky police officers knocking on your door. But to achieve this, you need to have your wits about you, which is something that many hapless hoodlums don't have.

Crims can leave their fingerprints behind; they can leave their wallets, their weapons, and even their false teeth. Huh? Real dumb crims cause utter chaos. They leave a trail of destruction behind them, crashing and burning as they go. Footprints in the snow, trails of broken glass ... Yep, police love those little tell-tale signs.

WHAT A PORKY!

Three mates went out bush, drank too much alcohol, started getting hungry, and realised they'd forgotten to bring food. One of them declared he wanted a barbecue, which seemed like a good idea at the time. So they all jumped in a ute and sped off at about twice the legal speed limit.

They drove 10 kilometres until they came to a pig farm. In their inebriated state, they decided that this was just the place to find a nice juicy hunk of meat to barbecue. One of the men scaled the fence and tied the end of a rope to the biggest pig he could find; the other two started pulling the 200-kilogram beast. The struggle was too much for a chain-link fence and a section collapsed with a crash, sending the other pigs into a stampede. Fearing for their lives, the three mates quickly hoisted the stolen pig up into the ute. They strapped it onto the back of the ute and sped away. Two kilometres down the road, the pig began making such a commotion that the ute started to swerve wildly.

The pig was thrown from the back of the ute and dragged along the dirt road for a kilometre.

Trying to take control, the driver ran off the road, and the ute rolled for 30 metres; all three men were thrown from the vehicle. Early the next morning, a passing motorist came upon an odd sight—three men with various seriously broken bones and an enormous—relatively unscathed—pig.

CAN'T PUT A FOOT WRONG

One night a man in a stolen wheelchair rolled up to an expensive shoe store, threw a brick through the window, got out of the wheelchair, and snuck inside. After gathering a few top-of-the-range Italian shoes, he awkwardly made his way back through the broken glass to his wheelchair, cutting his feet badly in the process. When he sat back in the wheelchair, one of the tyres instantly burst due to punctures from the glass all over the ground. So the man left the wheelchair and hobbled off down the street. Police followed the bloody footprints and found their shoe thief still carrying the shoes. That's when it hit him ... they were all right-foot shoes!

COVER YOUR TRACKS!

Police were called to a convenience store early one morning after a report of a burglar alarm going off. They arrived to find a side door broken. A witness said she had seen two men in dark clothing using a rope to drag an ATM from the shop. She had watched them and was able to tell police that the pair went through an alley toward some apartments. Police had little trouble finding the suspected apartment. After obtaining a search warrant, they entered and found the ATM sitting right next to the front door. The thieves were amazed that they had been tracked down and asked police how they knew where they were. It had literally been a treasure trail and all the police had to do was follow the clues scattered along the footpath and up the stairwell—piles of dropped coins, light globes for the neon sign on the ATM, a phone cord, and a sign that said 'ATM'.

THIRD TIME UNLUCKY?

A man who lived just up the road from a pub decided to break in one night and get himself a free TV set. Everything went smoothly, so he decided to have a second go, and later that week he broke in again and scored himself a dozen bottles of alcohol. Starting to think it was all too easy, he had a go for the third time using the same modus operandi—getting inside through the roof. This time, however, he lost his footing, fell to the floor in a spray of glass, and accidentally shot himself in the foot. Stunned and sheepish, he went home in the dark without stealing anything. He was surprised to find the police at his door a short time later. In the darkness, he had failed to notice that he had left a trail of blood all the way to his doorstep!

MONEY TO BURN

A bunch of crooks were over the moon; they had just made one of the biggest hauls ever—over $18 million. What they did was hold-up an armoured car and force it to drive into isolated bushland. They had the cash, they'd escaped, and no one knew where they were ... what could possibly be better?

The next step was to actually get at the goods and open the back of the armoured vehicle. How did they do it? By using high-powered acetylene torches with a bit too much enthusiasm. The operation started an horrific fire, destroying the armoured car, burning all the money to a crisp, and forcing our criminal masterminds to run for their lives in utter terror.

SQUASHED DOUGHNUTS AIN'T PRETTY

A delivery van was parked at a convenience store with its engine running while a delivery man carried doughnuts inside. You can guess what happened next. Two guys who had spent the afternoon smoking crack decided to hop in and go for a doughnut joy-ride. What they hadn't noticed was that the rear doors were wide open.

Going way over the speed limit as they raced along, they left a 15-kilometre trail of doughnuts behind them. They abandoned the van when they were spotted by police responding to reports of a dangerous driver who was losing his doughnuts ... and maybe his marbles as well.

WHAT CASH REGISTER?

Police arrived at a local deli at 10.00 p.m. one Wednesday night in response to a security alarm. The front door was smashed and clearly, one of the suspects had cut his hand and was bleeding badly. Police found that the cash register had been disconnected from the counter and removed. A description was sent out and immediately a responding unit came back on the radio stating that a small car with three suspects was seen heading north, boot open, cash register in plain view.

Police tracked down the car and pulled them over. It was quite obvious they weren't intelligentsia. The cash register was too big to fit in the boot, so they had tried to tie it closed with a torn blood-soaked T-shirt. Secondly, they hadn't taken any money from the cash drawer so what little money was left was merrily blowing out of the open boot, leaving a trail of coins and notes along the road. But they deserve some credit for quick thinking. When asked where they were going with the cash register, the deadpan driver replied, 'What cash register?'

BUDDY, CAN YOU SPARE A BUD?

A man decided to shoplift six stubbies of Budweiser beer and, for some obscure reason, decided to keep hold of one and stuff the other five down his cargo pants.

The store manager noticed him walking out the door holding his one stubby and looking a little unsteady on his feet. He called out to him, assuming he'd just forgotten to pay. When he didn't respond, the manager tried to stop him leaving. That's when it got interesting.

The beer-loving shoplifter went on the rampage and started kicking the manager. At this, all the other bottles started falling out of his pants, smashing to pieces all over the floor. To get out of the mess, the man ran outside straight towards the nearest car. The female driver looked aghast at the sight of a desperate, dishevelled man lunging towards her and took off, leaving him stranded.

To top it all off, when arrested, the shoplifter gave police a false name. But it wasn't 'false' at all ... it was in fact his brother's real name and real address.

SMASHING GOOD TIME

A man walked into a liquor shore at around 10.30 p.m. and selected two six-packs of Budweiser beer. Cool as a cucumber, he gave the shop assistant a cheesy grin and walked out the door. Once outside, he seems to have lost his cool. He tripped on the step and fell down, smashing most of the beer bottles. Picking himself up, he made a run for it. As he ran through a dark lane, he crashed into a young woman who happened to be carrying a bottle of wine from the same store. He managed to cause yet another accident, this time slashing his arm on a shard of glass. Police arrested him at his home nearby smelling of beer, white wine and blood.

WHY BUY WHEN YOU CAN STEAL?

One morning a man who worked at a tile retailer got to work only to discover that the tiling display was missing, as were three plastic palm trees used for decoration. The man didn't need to be a super sleuth to find them ... there was a trail of dirt up the street leading to a house about 100 metres away. The trail of dirt led around the side of the house to the back garden where—lo and behold!—there was a newly paved barbeque area with three plastic palm trees sur-rounded by dozens of odd ill-matching pavers.

YOU COULD TRY AND
COVER YOUR TRACKS!

A man was caught shoplifting. He and his haul were carted off to the local police station for questioning and he was released later that day. The next morning, the police chief came to work and found some-one had thrown a rock through the police station window and broken in. Incredibly the thief had ignored computer equipment, ammunition, radios and other valuable items. What they did take was a small cardboard box containing the items the thief had been accused of shoplifting the previous day. Not so incredibly, police had a strong suspicion as to the identity of this brainless second-time-unlucky thief.

CLEAN YOUR SHOES!

A man involved in a betting shop hold-up happened to have dog poo on the soles of his shoes. Police used enhanced photos from a security camera to match the pattern of excrement found at the crime scene to that of his shoe. We won't record what he said when he was found out.

DON'T STEAL A COMPUTER FROM A COMPUTER NUT

A fellow who had 33 burglary convictions under his belt was staggering home, dead drunk, when he had a brainwave—why not pick a random house and swipe something? So he did, and once inside the house he saw a nice computer that he could use. Unbeknownst to him, the homeowner was a very security-conscious software developer. He worked at home and had been robbed three times before of valuable documentation and files, so he had put together a foolproof anti-theft system with several hidden security cameras linked up to his private website.

When our bungling robber entered the house, a motion detector kicked on, and several cameras placed strategically around the house caught our hero in action. The pictures were then automatically sent to the owner's website.

The owner was overseas at the time of the burglary, but that didn't matter. When he logged on to his website he saw the interior shots of his house with the contents in disarray, and he got excellent footage of the thief in action. With the tap-tap-tap of a computer keyboard, he sent off some very good pictures to the police who, faster than you can say Windows 2000, were able to identify the mystery thief. Thirty-three burglary convictions? Make that 34.

YOU BIG DRIP!

A man was arrested for stealing a commercial paint sprayer after leaving a 300-metre trail of green paint to his front yard.

SNOW DOWN SHOWDOWN!

Three men wearing ski masks robbed a bank—well, at least they remembered to wear masks, because everything else they did made it really easy for the police to track them down. Since there was fresh snow on the ground, responding units tracked the villains footsteps across a vacant lot to an apartment block. Fresh snow from the suspects' boots led to an open apartment door. Once inside, police found a pad next to the telephone with a sketch of the route to and from the bank, as well as the phone number of a local taxi company. Easy as pie, the police ascertained from the taxi company that they had picked up three men and got the address to where they were heading. Police were ready to greet them when they hopped out of the taxi outside a bar.

TICKER TAPE PARADE

A taxi driver noticed a couple of hoons breaking into an electrical warehouse early one morning. He called the police and when they arrived, they discovered that the front door had been kicked in and the cash register had been stolen. Yep, they'd ripped it right out of the wall. Unfortunately for our mad muscle men, they didn't realise that as they ran away, the cash register tape was unrolling behind them. The police simply followed the 40-metre trail of tape into the nearby bushes where they found two men hiding. It all happened so quickly, they didn't have time to come up with a convincing explanation of what they were doing. Pity, it would have been a doozey!

LET'S BE AS UNOBTRUSIVE AS POSSIBLE

When they couldn't get it open, two men decided to steal a whopping big safe—all three tonnes of it! They tied it to the back of their truck and headed off down the street. The metal scraping against the asphalt caused a deafening roar and a massive shower of sparks that could be seen for blocks away. Unfortunately for them, several witnesses along the way reported the strange sight to police.

MAL AIN'T HERE!

It was snowing heavily when a tracker arrived with his dog to follow-up a burglary. A police officer and the tracker set off with the dog. The dog quickly picked up the scent of the offender across an open field right up to one particular home owned by a man called 'Mal'. The police officer had dealt with 'Mal' many times before; it seemed like he was a likely candidate for the break-in.

When they came to the front door of the house, they found it was unlocked. The dog's reaction was very strong; he was excited, scratching at the door, and whining relentlessly. Once inside, it was clear they were near the end of their search—there were fresh snow tracks towards the back of the house. The dog quickly ran through to the back of the house and stuck his head under a bed in the furthest bedroom. The dog would not come out from under the bed. The police officer went up to the bed and said quietly, 'Come on out, Mal'. From under the bed came the reply: 'Mal ain't here.'

IMPRESSIVE ESCAPE

In the early afternoon, two police officers pulled over a known offender driving a pick-up truck with a suspended licence. As the officers were preparing to issue a ticket, the suspect revved the truck, put it in gear, and roared down the road. That's when the 'fun' began! One officer was struck by the truck's side-view mirror; the other only just managed to jump out of the way before the guy drove over his motorbike, totally crushing it to pieces. Minutes later a third officer in a car began a pursuit but ended it after a few minutes because it had become too dangerous. Respite in the fight against crime? No!

About two hours later the unoccupied truck was located outside a hotel. As officers surrounded the hotel, the suspect jumped out a window and ran towards a nearby highway. A police dog tracker team arrived just as the suspect scaled the three-metre highway fence. As he jumped down the other side of the fence, it appeared that he was once again going to elude police. Instead of continuing with his short-lived freedom, the suspect turned back and began kicking dirt through the fence and into the dog's face, gloating and mocking the police on the other side of the wire. Laughing, he turned, ran across the eight-lane highway and was immediately struck by a car, breaking his right leg, and causing multiple injuries including a punctured lung. Was that enough? Nooooo! With a broken leg and one working lung, he made it across the highway and limped towards a river. While seriously injured, he found a perfect hiding place in dense bushes on the river's bank.

Meanwhile the tracker team was on the trail ... and doggy was a tad angry from being so rudely kicked at. With his nostrils still full of dirt and gravel, that dog came closer and closer until a small part of the suspect could be seen between the bushes ... the section from the his bellybutton down to mid-thigh. Wham! The dog located and attacked his target. Yep, right between the legs! Dog one; idiot zero.

ROBINSON CRUSOE THEY AIN'T

If you're going for a boat ride, it really helps to know the local geography. Three teenagers stole a boat, beached it, and then set fire to it in an act of mindless vandalism. What these creative minds failed to realise was that they were on an island. Several hours later, a helicopter team was called in to rescue the boys who faced some rather awkward questioning from police along the lines of: 'So what happened to the boat?'

AGRO GETS YOU NOWHERE

A 26-year-old man thought he had a pretty good plan to get some free cigarettes, but his plan had a few minor flaws. It all started when he went into a convenience store and walked out with three cartons of cigarettes, in full view of the shop assistant, at about 1.00 a.m. one Thursday morning. When he got back to his car, he found he had locked himself out and couldn't find the keys. Then he noticed that the pesky shop assistant had followed him outside to confront him.

Our key-less thief told the man that it was just a joke and he didn't intend to steal the cigarettes, but the shop assistant didn't believe him, went back inside, and called the police. The police station, by the way, was just across the road .

Our thief was by this time in quite a bad temper. He stormed back into the store and ripped out the telephone for revenge. Then he grabbed $50 from the till and stormed out again. He now had some cash to go with his cigarettes, but that still left the problem of the locked getaway car. What to do?

For the third time that night, the frazzled shop assistant watched as the stranded thief came back into the store and grabbed a broom. Dispatchers watched from the police station across the road as the man used the broom to smash a window on his vehicle. Finally, he drove off, only to run into an oncoming police car moments later. He fled the car, fell into a ditch, and his exasperating night came to a humiliating end.

HERE I AM ...
COME AND GET ME, OFFICER!

A red car came to a screeching halt outside a convenience store early one afternoon. The car was in a really bad state, as if it had just been involved in an accident. A dazed young man stumbled in and asked to use the phone. He explained in breathless tones that he needed to call the police because someone had pulled a hit-and-run on him. Sure enough, the young man grabbed the phone and dialled the police. But even before he had finished speaking, two police cars pulled up outside. It turns out the police had been searching for his very car. There was no hit-and-run, but a string of drink-driving offences including hitting a fence, driving through three front gardens, and running into the side of a house. Searching him and the car, they came up with some further evidence to charge him with—a nice tidy stash of cocaine.

LIKE A RAT IN A MAZE

A wealthy homeowner with a passion for art had what he thought was a burglar-proof property—that was, until a burglar who loved a challenge figured out a way to get in. The only problem was that he couldn't figure out a way to get out!

The story begins when the burglar squeezed in through a small vent in the roof and proceeded to tumble six metres to the floor (the homeowner had high ceilings!). Picking himself up, he took a good look around and noted some luxury items that were just waiting to be stolen. Then he checked out his exit options and this is where his troubles began. As he hobbled around from door to door, he realised he was leaving a trail of blood, but there wasn't much he could do about it. Then he found all the doors were locked with custom-made deadlocks. It was then that a deafening din began—both the fire alarm and the security alarm went off simultaneously. Eeee-ooo-eeee-oooo! The fire brigade arrived, the police arrived, and he wished he could leave.

When a representative from the security firm arrived the next day to make the vent burglar-proof again and install motion sensors, the cleaning crew were hard at it ... steam cleaning the poor blood-soaked carpet.

BUMBLING BANDIT

Waiting in line at an ATM, a man figured that he had a foolproof way to get a few extra bucks. As the customer in front of him completed her transaction and received her money from the machine, our brilliant thief demanded she hand it over. Instead of giving him the money, the customer bolted inside the bank to report the crime.

The thief panicked and ran out onto the street. Here he spotted a man sitting in his car. He tried it again: 'Give me all your money!' The frightened man said he only had $10 but he handed it over anyway. The thief, now with the grand sum of $10 in two $5 notes, raced off down the road, realising he needed to get out of the area quick before the police arrived. He ran out into the street and flagged down a passing car. No, it wasn't a police car! But as the car came to a stop, the driver opened his window and our thief held out one of the $5 notes telling the driver he would give him it to him if he gave him a ride. The driver grabbed the money and sped away, leaving the thief standing in the middle of the street minus five bucks.

In his final attempt to leave the scene, our unlucky crim spotted a city bus pulling up to a nearby bus stop. He jumped on the bus, convinced that he had finally put his problems behind him. But his trail of misfortune had been noted by several bank customers and employees, who were able to give police the exact number, direction, and location of the bus. Finally, he managed to get a ride ... to jail.

WALK THIS WAY!

An armed man robbed a taxi driver and then escaped on foot. One foot, to be exact. From the crime scene it was clear that the man's gun had accidentally discharged and he had shot himself in the foot. All police had to do was follow the trail of bloody footprints.

JUST ROB A BANK NEXT TIME!

Two criminal masterminds were attempting to break into a safe to get at whatever goodies might be hiding inside. After failing to pick the lock, they decided to blast the safe open with dynamite. The explosion destroyed most of the room, but the safe was left totally unscathed. So what could they do next? Since they were up on the second floor, they decided to shove the safe out the window—a foolproof way to break it open. But no such luck. So the dynamic duo, realising that their time was running out, thought they would drag the safe away to somewhere where they would have more time to work it open. So, they ran a chain from the safe to the back of their pick-up truck and set off. As they headed down the road at a rapid pace with their booty in tow, they came to a traffic light, which turned red just as they were approaching. The driver slammed on the brakes quickly; luckily their pick-up had good brakes, but the safe didn't. The safe rammed the rear of the truck, lifting the back off the ground and lodging itself underneath. This pretty well brought this little heist to a close.

THERE'S A HOLE IN MY POCKET

A teenager robbed his local convenience store and scored himself two pockets full of cash. He didn't realise that he had holes in both of his pockets ... and a trail of small change led police directly to his doorstep.

FOOT IN MOUTH

Criminals who say the wrong thing at the wrong time!

In the movies, criminal masterminds are always clear thinking and articulate with razor-sharp wit. They may not be particularly charming, but they can hold their own at any swank dinner party; they can dazzle their audiences with amusing repartee; and they never commit a faux pas.

On the other hand, dumb crooks are always putting their foot in their mouth. Sometimes it's during the robbery; sometimes it's after, but it always leads to their downfall. Criminals so often say the wrong thing at the wrong time ... Best to keep your mouth shut!

WHERE WERE YOU ON THE NIGHT OF ... ?

A man was arrested because police suspected that he had robbed a jewellery store. The man swore he did not do it. When the police asked if he had an alibi, he explained that he had been busy breaking into a school at the same time. Bingo! Police dropped the jewellery store charges and arrested him for breaking into the school.

DID I SAY THAT?

A man rang police to report a break-in, which seems to have happened while he was at work. Police showed up. It was a wealthy neighbourhood and the victim was clearly not struggling to make a living. The police walked around to the side of the house where the man showed them where the burglars must have gained entry by prising open a sliding glass door. When asked if anything in the house was missing, the man said nothing except his stash of marijuana. Police, not believing what they had just heard, asked him to repeat himself. The man, realising his faux pas, stuttered and stammered and finally waved the police away with an embarrassed, 'Oh, let's just forget the whole thing.' The police walked away, laughing.

GREAT EXPLANATIONS OF OUR TIME

An 18-year-old was shot three times while selling crack. Five days after leaving the hospital, he was back in business. He got pulled over for a burned out light on the back of his jeep. As the police officer approached, he smelled the distinct aroma of marijuana, so he asked the guy to exit the vehicle. As he got out, 47 rocks of crack fell to the ground.

'Is that what I think it is?' the officer asked.

'I don't know,' our clueless jeep driver replied. 'Must have been something in my lap.'

A FEAT WITH A FOOT!

Loose lips sink ships and drunk friends can really spill the beans. One is cursing his mate 'Chip' for what he once did in a hotel. Sitting down with a new group of friends, Chip had way too much to drink and began telling them a strange tale ... all about a man who got away with insurance fraud. An off-duty police officer in the group was most interested to hear all the details ... and, boy, were they gory! It seems that Chip's friend wanted to cash-in the $500 000 from his insurance policy. He told the insurance company that he had lost his left foot in a motorbike accident, but what he actually did was get two mates—including Chip—to chop off his left foot with a hatchet. Surely there are less painful ways to make an insurance claim.

POSITIVE IDENTIFICATION

A purse-snatcher grabbed a young woman's bag as she left a clothing store. The shop assistant called police immediately and both of them were able to give the police a fairly detailed description of the culprit. Circling the block a few minutes later, the police had no trouble finding their suspect. He was picked up for questioning and driven back to the store. He was then taken out of the car and told to stand there for a positive ID, to which he replied, 'Yes officer, that's her. That's the lady I stole the purse from.'

GREAT DIALOGUE OF OUR TIME

Officer: What is your DOB?
Criminal: What's a DOB, man?
Officer: When's your birthday?
Criminal: Fifth of May
Officer: What year?
Criminal: Every year, man.

BUT OFFICER, I WASN'T THERE!

A man called Crime Stoppers to report a crime so he could collect the reward money. He was helpful, polite, and a mine full of information about the crime. So much so, that the police put two and two together and realised that he had actually committed it. Standard procedure calls for authorities to take down the caller's name and address, which they did. And wasn't he surprised when half and hour later a police car showed up outside his place to pick him up.

WHICH ONE'S THE IDIOT?

It's good to try and fade into anonymity in a police line-up, but one clever clod just couldn't help himself. When detectives asked each man in the line-up to repeat the words: 'Give me all your money or I'll shoot', our golden boy shouted, 'That's not what I said!'

WRONG SIDE OF THE BARS!

One late shift at about 4.30 a.m., an officer passed the entrance to a local bar and noticed a man sitting on the stairs inside of the security grille, fiddling with the lock on the gate. The police officer kindly asked whether he could help and the man said, 'Yes! Help me get out of here before the cops come!' The officer told the young man that he would be right back and the man was encouraged by his offer of assistance. 'I'll give you half of what I got! Just get me out of here!' he promised. Help arrived in the form of police backup, but the man was by then so intoxicated that he had forgotten where he was or how he had broken in to the bar in the first place. And he certainly had no idea that he'd been dealing with a uniformed police officer. Well, he'll have plenty of time to reflect upon it in the cool, quiet solitude of his cell!

NICE TRY, SHAME ABOUT YOUR BIG MOUTHS!

A young man got a job at one of the sawmills in a small town. With his hard-earned cash he went out and bought a fancy White Toyota four-wheel-drive vehicle with roll bars, light bar, fancy stereo, chrome wheels and so on. His credit wasn't very good, so the interest rate was pretty high. He also had a few speeding tickets, so insurance wasn't cheap. Needless to say, the loser lost his job. He didn't have any way to make the payments so he and his cousin came up with a brilliant plan over quite a few beers—they were going to push the four-wheel-drive down a hill and claim the insurance.

So, off they went. They drove to a lookout, put the car in neutral, gave it a great heave, and off it rolled ... but it only travelled a few metres before rolling into a juniper bush. The second time they did a brilliant job. The vehicle toppled down the steep hillside, bouncing off trees and boulders, before bounding across the road at the bottom of the hill and going into the river. Yes sir! Mission accomplished.

Since the fraudsters no longer had wheels, they had to walk down the hill back to town and by this time it was dark. They were drunk and tired and fell over numerous times. Scratched, bruised and covered with dirt, they managed to avoid the police at the bottom of the hill, and went to the nearest watering hole and called the police to report their 'stolen' vehicle. While they were waiting for the police to come and take a statement, they decided to have a few more beers and plan on what to do with the insurance money. As we all know, alcohol seems to increase the confidence and verbal decibels of the drinker, and by the next day the whole town knew what those two boys had done.

GUILTY YOUR HONOUR!

A car thief drove a stolen vehicle straight to a police station to confess. His unexpected guilty conscience stunned grateful officers who did not even know the roadside heist had occurred. As the conscience-stricken 22-year-old was arrested, he explained, 'Someone put me up to it'. Adjourning the case to a later date, the judge told him, 'Frankly, you are an idiot and I hope you realise that.'

WRONG ADDRESS, STUPID!

Very few thieves plan ahead. Here's one who did, so he should get some credit. But then again, maybe not ... A novice bank robber was planning to hold-up a local department store that was part of a statewide chain. As part of his scintillating pre-planning stage, the thief called police to report a robbery taking place in another store across town just prior to making his move. In this way, he figured the police would all set off across town to the wrong location, leaving him free to pull off his cunning plan. And the plan might have worked, too, except for one thing. Instead of giving them the address of the store across town, he stuffed up and gave them the address of the store he was going to rob. The result? A thief halfway through carrying out the robbery of a lifetime is rudely interrupted by a swarm of patrol cars. Gulp!

ONLY JOKING, OFFISHER!

A police officer was driving home from work and stopped at a corner store to pick up some milk. While walking back to his car, a blue Chevrolet swerved across the street, mounted the kerb, and careered into the passenger side of his car. The officer's first reaction was to check whether the driver of the car was all right. His second reaction was to let rip at the idiot for wrecking his car. But as he went over to the driver's seat, a lanky, shaken man got out of the vehicle, handed the officer a quarter-full bottle of whisky and said, 'Quick, get rid of this before the cops come, will ya?' The officer took the bottle from him, as requested, and watched the look of relief on his face slowly transform into horror when he realised just who he was talking to ... a police officer in full uniform!

PLANNING AHEAD

If only all criminals set their plans well in advance ... One Monday, police got a call from an employee of a small phone company which sells mobile phones and call plans. An ex-employee had rung an old mate who still worked there and told him to leave the doors unlocked and the cash out from the day's sales so that he could come and take it. Police staked out the building, and sure enough, at 1.00 a.m. that night, the very trusting thief approached the store where the door had been conveniently left open, according to plan. Police watched him enter the building and search around for a few minutes, then they moved in. All in all, the surveillance team had quite an easy morning's work.

A BIG HELLO FROM KEN'S HOUSE!

Let's make this story clear by giving these three men names. There's the thief Dave, the friend Robbo, and the victim, Ken. Dave stole $2300 worth of XBox games, speakers and DVDs from Ken, an acquaintance he had met through his friend Robbo. Content with his stash, he then made himself at home, had a drink, watched some TV and used Ken's phone to ring his mate, Robbo. Dave wasn't so stupid to spill the beans about the robbery, but he did mention that he was over at Ken's place. After a bit of a chat, Robbo hung up the phone and wondered why on earth Dave would be at Ken's place in the middle of the day. So he rang up Ken. It just didn't seem right and it wasn't—police arrested Dave later that day.

KEEP YOUR MOUTH SHUT

A police chase ended when the suspect crashed into a stationary car. No-one was injured. The police officer and suspect headed to the police station in the police car while the suspect's car was towed away. The suspect was quite concerned about his car and asked what would happen to it. The police officer assured him that it would be held securely until the man paid for the towing bill. 'Phew!' the suspect said with relief. 'I can handle the driving charges but I'm glad you didn't find the cocaine.'

A CASE OF PERFORMANCE ANXIETY?

A robber leapt from a car. He ran up the front steps of a bank wearing a fierce black mask with his gun held high. As he kicked the door open, he tripped on the last step and his mask fell off. As he attempted to pick himself up off the ground, his foot got tangled in the doormat and he slid across the floor towards the counter. Staggering to his feet, all he wanted was to get the robbery over and done with, so he waved his fake gun menacingly in the air, glared at the bemused bank teller and roared, 'This is a stuff-up!'

'THIS IS A ... WHAT?'

'Up with your fucking hands, this is a stick-up!' Sounds good, thought the nervous young robber as he went through the planned robbery in his head, because mental preparation is everything with a job like this. Mask on, jump out of car, run into the bank, wave the gun in the air and shout, 'Up with your fucking hands, this is a stick-up!' Good. He was ready.

Half an hour later, the young man and his accomplice roared up to the bank. The man put on his mask, jumped out of the car, and did exactly what he'd been planning. Except that in his nervous state he yelled out, 'Up with your sticky hands, this is a fuck-up!' After a short pause, it was clear that one of the bank tellers was trying to stop himself from laughing. Another startled chuckling, and another, until all the tellers and customers were laughing. The would-be robber was so humiliated that he zipped out of the bank amidst the chuckling. Mission not accomplished.

IT'S A SIN TO TELL A LIE!

A police officer saw a suspicious character lurking around a bishop's residence at an unusually late hour. The man denied he was doing anything wrong but was found to have the bishop's wallet in his possession. He was brought in for questioning and the police called the bishop. Sure enough, his wallet was missing and the bishop confirmed there was about $260 in it. When police put this to the suspect, he became very indignant and blurted out, 'I thought bishops didn't lie! He only had $180!'

BIG MOUTH!

A man was brought in for questioning by police in connection with an alleged traffic infringement. When police told him that he knew why he was there, he said he did ... and proceeded to confess to 40 burglaries that police had not even connected to him!

SMALL TIME BUNGLES

*Why rob a bank when
you can stuff up somewhere else?*

It's nice to think that crooks attempt great things, but sometimes it's just not the case. So many crooks bungle the simplest break-in. They get the wrong house, the wrong victim, they fall asleep on the job, or they forget what they came for. Some hopeful souls remain too persistent when all they should do is stop — like the guy who broke into a house and stuck around long enough to play a Beethoven sonata. Others just don't have what it takes and run out of steam when they suffer their first setback — like when the shop assistant they're trying to hold up bursts out laughing in their face. Sure, crime can be exhilarating and enthralling, but sometimes it's just plain humiliating. Small-time bunglers of the criminal world, we salute you!

EATING OUT IS SO EXPENSIVE THESE DAYS

A man was asleep in his upstairs bedroom when he heard noises coming from his kitchen. He went downstairs to investigate and saw an unknown man helping himself to some barbecue chicken. He called police who arrived to find the man with a plate full of chicken bones. The man claimed he knew the resident, but when police asked him what his name was he shrugged and said, 'Well, you got me.' He was charged with trespassing and fined $1087 for petty larceny, which would pay for a hell of a lot of barbecue chickens!

EASY MONEY

A postal worker saw a good way to make some money—he fudged records and stole a money order made out for several hundred dollars.

Perhaps his master plan needed a bit more thought. You see he made the money order out to himself, cashed it at the bank next door, and deposited the money into his own savings account. It took investigators all of 30 minutes to wrap up the case.

DON'T TRUST THE LOCALS!

A middle-aged tourist was watching the sunset at an island resort when he was befriended by a young man and woman. They invited him back to their place to see what a typical islander home and family looked like. The man was happy to tag along, thinking he was in for a lovely cross-cultural evening. Once they were back home, they encouraged our trusting middle-aged man to take a sponge bath as a token of traditional island hospitality. Relaxed and happy, he got back to his hotel room to discover his passport, traveller's cheques, and $520 cash had mysteriously vanished from his trouser pocket. He had been ripped off. Only later did it occur to him that he knew exactly where they lived ...

WHY DO THEY KEEP RUNNING AWAY?

A young man entered a small suburban supermarket, walked up to a checkout lane, and quietly told the cashier he had a gun. She shrieked and ran to the back of the store. Undaunted, he walked to the next lane and told this cashier the same thing; she screamed even louder and headed off to join her friend. Mr Persistence kept at it and tried a third cashier. You guessed it—she did what the others did. With no more checkout lanes open, what did he do? He decided to steal $50 from the pharmacy next door, except that in all the confusion, there was plenty of time for the police to pull up quietly out the front ...

A CLEAN GETAWAY?

They do say a clean car is a happy car, don't they? Two car thieves stole a Honda that was parked on the street outside someone's house. Maybe they had impossibly high standards for cleanliness, because instead of getting the hell out of there, they took it to a car wash.

And not a car wash some distance away, but the neighborhood car wash just around the corner.

The owner of the Honda happened to be passing by when he noticed his car waiting in line to be washed. He called the cops on his mobile phone and they arrived when the car emerged from its deluxe wash and wax.

THIRTY DAYS HATH SEPTEMBER ...

A police officer pulled over a vehicle that ran a red light. It didn't have numberplates but there was an official looking Department of Motor Vehicles sticker on the rear window, which caught the police officer's eye. He ran a check and found the car was stolen and so was the Department of Motor Vehicles sticker. The police officer had suspected as much when he noticed that the suspect had dutifully filled in the bogus expiry date of '31 April'.

BUT OFFICER, SHE'S PSYCHIC!

A bank clerk came up with a great scheme to make heaps of money. His girlfriend worked on a psychic hotline where she was paid according to how long she could keep customers on the line. So when he got to work in the morning, he would dial up his girlfriend's number and leave the phone off the hook until he left for the day. Who was stupider—the bank, who didn't notice the outrageous telephone bills until five months and $163 000 later, or the psychic pair who didn't see their luck was running out?

KEEP YOUR EYES OPEN

A man was picked up by police for questioning about a recent theft. With a search warrant in hand, they went with him to his apartment and had a look around. It was while they were looking for evidence that our covetous thief noticed the investigating officer's glasses—very chic designer specs. So, as he bid the police a fond farewell, he managed to grab them right out of the police car. And he got away with it too ... until the officer found she needed them. The police car did a quick U-turn, and the police officers dropped in again. Not just a suspect for theft now, he was under arrest!

NO HOLIDAY PAY EITHER, BOZO!

A 16-year-old left school and got a job at a newsagency. One morning, the store manager dropped by unannounced and found him scratching a stack of not yet purchased scratchies in full view of the customers. When confronted, he just shrugged calmly, took the pile of scratchies, and went away. The manager called the police and they arrived a short time later to get a full written report. With impeccable timing, the young guy came back. To apologise? To return the instant lotto tickets? No, he asked for his pay cheque! He didn't get it. He really didn't get it ...

GO ON, GIVE US A SMILE!

A 19-year-old computer whiz-kid was arrested for drink driving and was summoned to appear in court. When he arrived at the police station for the hearing, he found a computer just sitting there and noone around. Deciding to have a bit of fun, he broke into the database and deleted his file from the hard drive.

When the police officer went to access his file, all she found was a smiley face. Apparently, the powers that be failed to see the funny side. The man was given a three-month suspended sentence, fined $425, and lost his licence.

PLEASE CHECK THE
NUMBER BEFORE DIALLING

At 3.00 a.m. one morning, a man was awakened by his telephone ringing. Thinking it was urgent news, he answered it, but found that it was a rambling obscene phone call by someone who was clearly drunk. The man called police on his mobile phone and tried to keep the caller talking so that they would be able to trace the call. During that time, the caller fell asleep while still on the phone and began to snore. By the time police tracked him down, they arrived to find him asleep on his couch, phone in hand and the line still open. And the strangest thing about this? The drunken caller had dialled a random number, which happened to belong to a police chief. The odds of randomly dialling a particular police officer is about one in 10 million. In fact, you're more likely to become parents of quadruplets or die from falling out of bed!

'DO NOT DISTURB'

Thinking of robbing a furniture store? Get enough sleep the night before! A cleaner in a major furniture showroom got a surprise early one morning when she went to clean the staff toilet ... there was a pistol lying on the counter. Then she heard strange noises coming from across the showroom in the bedroom display. Nervously, she tiptoed over and found a would-be thief snoring his heart out, blissfully asleep on the display bed. The man was irritated at being woken by police and told officers, 'Hey, I was asleep!'

BEER? WHAT BEER?

Two cops in an unmarked vehicle went to investigate a party that was getting out of hand with a lot of under-age drinking. When they pulled up to the premises, they were greeted by the 'host' DJ, who had amazingly loud amplifiers and speakers. To the cops' amusement, his voice rang out loud and clear as they arrived: 'HIDE THE BEER! THE COPS ARE HERE! HIDE THE BEER!' Mr Host had forgotten that he was broadcasting live to everyone within hearing distance ... what more evidence did the cops need?

HOLY SMOKE!

A police officer spotted a man standing by a fence smoking with his pants down about to urinate. When the officer shouted, the man yanked up his pants, shoved his cigarette into his pocket and took off ... but the cigarette was alight! With his pants on fire, the man ran down the road followed by the police officer yelling for him to hit the ground. Trailing smoke and ashes, our smoky hero kept going until his trousers slipped down around his ankles and tripped him up. The police officer dived on top of him, slapping out the fire, but the man continued to try and get away, punching and kicking, until another officer arrived and cut away the burning pants. There's one to tell the grandchildren!

TESTING, TESTING, ONE TWO THREE ...

A man, who we can confidently say is not the brightest star in the sky, decided to steal some beer from his neighbour's garage. He made his move at 4.00 p.m. one sunny Saturday afternoon—just the time when his neighbour was at home. Wearing a backpack to carry the beer, he climbed the fence and entered through the back door of the garage. The owner heard a noise and decided to investigate since beer had been stolen from his refrigerator before. He walked in and came face-to-face with his neighbour and a backpack suspiciously full of beer bottles. A chase ensued, with the owner catching his neighbour and crash tackling him onto the road. He struggled, kicking and punching the homeowner, even spraying him in the face with mace, but the owner managed to hold him down on the pavement until his wife called the police.

Caught in the act with lots of broken beer bottles and proof of physical assault ... what more evidence do you need? Helpfully, the dumb crim had even more evidence for prosecutors to sift through— he had a mini cassette player in his pocket on which he had recorded a step-by-step narrative of his crime!

FIND A NEW GIRLFRIEND, STUPID!

A university student decided to pay for his drug habit by stealing CDs and video games from his girlfriend's brother and then selling them back to a CD store. However, there were three problems to his perfect crime: first he choose a local CD store where he was well-known; secondly, all the stolen goods had the owner's name on them; and thirdly, he signed his own name on the receipt he had to sign for the cash he received. Needless to say, now he has an ex-girlfriend.

MAYONNAISE WITH THAT?

Two men came into a sandwich shop and each ordered a sandwich. While they were being prepared, one of the men pulled out a knife and demanded cash. Instead of handing over the money, the quick-thinking employee set off an alarm and crash-tackled the man with the knife, sending it flying. The two would-be crooks got scared and ran from the shop. Did these bright buttons scoot and get away? Nah. The employee ran after them, yelling that he would give them the sandwiches for free if they came back. Police arrived as the pair of silly dufers sat patiently waiting for their lunchtime treat.

LOVE TO HELP

A man living next door to a car dealer heard noises late one night. He went out to see three men loading tyres onto the back of a truck. So being the neighbourly type, he went over and offered to help, explaining that he knew a police patrol car would be coming by pretty soon, so they needed to load up in a hurry. The man helped them load up the tyres, locked the back of the truck, and then pulled out his police badge.

WEAR A MASK NEXT TIME!

Here's a crime with a difference—a robbery plotted within full hearing range of the victim. A young man was filling out a job application at a hardware store when he overheard two other job applicants discussing a plan to rob him of his necklace and jacket. So he hid his necklace in his shoe and made a run for it. As they planned, the two men set off in pursuit, tackling him in the car park and making off with his jacket.

The victim was able to give police good descriptions of the men and their vehicle ... as they'd kindly left their names and addresses for police on their job applications!

DEAR BOB, LOVE BETTY

Police arrested 'Bob' the burglar while he was on the job. All they found in his possession was a big bag full of size 10 women's clothing. With a search warrant in hand, they headed for his house and looked around. Neat, tidy, quite ordinary except for the note they found on the kitchen counter:

'Dear Bob,
The washing machine broke down last night so we need another one. Could you steal one for us?
Love Betty
P.S. Could you ask Mum to clean the clothes you got for me?'

DO YOU WANT HAPPY SNAPPY

An experienced robber planned the perfect heist. He pulled out a gun on a couple of armoured car drivers, disarmed them, and made off with a few bags of cash. Problem was, he'd parked his getaway car next to a bus full of Japanese tourists. Fascinated by the robbery, the tourists snapped numerous pictures of the crook and his car. They were only too happy to share their photos with the police.

COULD SOMEONE GIVE ME A HAND?

A very obese man waddled into a jewellery store and ordered everyone to 'hit the floor'. Unfortunately, the would-be robber lost his balance and hit the floor himself, only he couldn't get up. Within minutes, a couple of kindly police officers helped him to his feet.

NIGHTY NIGHT!

Late one night, a drug addict broke into an elderly woman's home. Seeing a bottle of pills on her bedside table, he decided to sample a few. They happened to be Valium. He became drowsier and drowsier and fell asleep, leaving plenty of time for the woman to call police.

ISN'T SHE LUV-ER-LY?

The bride looked stunning in her very chic designer gown of ivory brocade. The happy couple were so proud that they sent their wedding photo to their local paper. But as soon as the local bridal boutique owner saw it, she recognised the couple and the dress—they had stolen it from her shop. It doesn't always pay to advertise.

CLIFF RICHARD SENT ME TO SLEEP!

A very tired thief broke into a CD warehouse and stole thousands of dollars worth of CD players, radios, cameras and plasma screen TVs. While waiting for his accomplices, he dozed off and was found the next morning by the manager, asleep in his office, with a Cliff Richard CD blasting from the speakers.

.WIMPS NOT WELCOME

'I have a gun. Give me $40', said the bank robber's note. But his intended victim, a female teller, looked up after reading the note, and said, 'Are you for real?' Taken aback, the robber nodded, but she didn't react. So after looking at her hopefully for a couple of seconds, he took his note and left. Perhaps you should ask for more next time and she might take you seriously.

KINKY!

A man came home from work to find evidence of an intruder—it seemed that someone had used his shower. On entering his bedroom, he was stunned to find the intruder asleep on his bed ... wearing his daughter's frilly pink underwear. On being rudely awakened, the highly inebriated intruder ran from the house into the nearby woods, clad in nothing except the rather unbecoming underpants. He was later found shivering in the bushes.

WHAT A LAUGH!

A service station attendant was working alone early one morning when a small, weedy man in a hooded sweatshirt came in and demanded money. She gave him the once-over and burst out laughing. Then in a stroke of genius, she explained that she was on the phone, talking to the police, so he'd better scoot. He did.

WORLD RECORD TIMING!

A police officer on a midnight shift patrol slammed on the brakes to avoid hitting a man who had run out in front of his patrol car. He recognised the man from previous petty offences, called him over, and began to haul him out for running in front of a car.

Just then, a radio call came through about a residential burglary where the suspect had fled the scene on foot. The address was exactly where the police officer had stopped his car ... and the man who was being shamed for nearly getting himself run over matched the description of the burglar.

The man heard the radio call, turned around and, before the police officer could say anything, offered his wrists to be handcuffed. Just then, the homeowner walked outside, still talking to police headquarters on her cordless phone. She positively identified him as the burglar—one of the speediest arrests on record!

DON'T MESS WITH THE MASSAGE!

Three men made appointments at a massage parlour for Saturday night. They had their massages and then forced the three women to hand over their takings. They thought it was such a good idea that they did it again at another massage parlour, and this time stole a mobile phone. After a good night's work, they sat down in a bar with a drink. The police tracked down the mobile phone number and gave the robbers a call. One of the men answered and because of the loud music in the background, it was clear they were in a bar or a nightclub. It wasn't a big city—the men were arrested before they had their second drink.

I'M FREE! I'M FREE! I'M ... OH

There's a minimum-security prison which is easy to walk out of. Most prisoners don't try it because it's surrounded by a mountain range on one side and desert on the others. One prisoner took his chances and escaped, with help from a fellow inmate, who drew him a map giving him directions over the mountain range and into the town on the other side.

After three days without food or water and fighting the harsh elements, the escapee finally crossed the mountain with relief ... only to discover that the 'town' was actually another minimum-security prison.

DOES THIS LOOK LIKE A BANK?

A man wearing a light-coloured shirt, shorts, sunglasses and gardening gloves attempted to hold-up two banks within 40 minutes—without much success! In the first attempt, he walked into a building through a set of automatic glass doors, and handed the woman behind the counter a note demanding cash. She consulted another employee and then handed the note back to him saying, 'Do you know you're in an instant print shop and all we can give you is photocopies?'

The man clearly wasn't totally embarrassed; he stayed long enough to inquire the whereabouts of the nearest bank. Employees gave him some vague directions and as soon as he left, called police.

Sure enough less than an hour later, a man wearing gardening gloves attempted to rob a bank nearby but, unfortunately for him, there were enough police on stand-by to make sure he didn't get very far.

ZILCH!

Police caught three men stealing an ATM outside a restaurant. Only problem was, it had been boarded up and out of order for two years!

DOES ANYONE HAVE THE KEY FOR THESE THINGS?

Father's Day. A 10-year-old boy wanted to be close to his dad—literally—so he took an old pair of handcuffs and locked himself to his father, wrist-to-wrist. It was a good joke ... until they couldn't find the key, so they called the police department. The officers came and had a good chuckle; Dad and his son thanked them for releasing them and everyone was happy, until officers returned minutes later and told the father that they had warrants for his arrest: a couple of minor charges, but warrants all the same. And so Dad was back in handcuffs—official police ones this time—and on his way to jail. 'I was hoping to spend more time with my kids on Father's Day,' the man said when he was released on Monday afternoon. 'So it was kind of ironic. And a little embarrassing.'

GOTCHA!

A service station proprietor called police. Three hundred dollars was missing from his cash register and he had all his employees remain at the station. When the police officer arrived, he lined up the four young employees, who were all between the ages of 17 and 19, and they were all looking a bit nervous. The police officer asked each of them in turn whether they had taken the money. No- one admitted to the theft. So the officer nodded slowly and then hit them with this, 'Well, in a few minutes I will know. Do you know why? Because the money has been treated with dye and when the thief's hands start to sweat, they'll turn bright blue'. Believable? Not really, but the youngest boy, hands at his side, immediately shot a glance down at his right hand. Sprung!

DUMB CROOK OR DUMB CHECKOUT CHICK?

Police were searching for a man with a sense of humour, who had paid for $150 worth of groceries with a bogus $200 note. He walked out of the store with his groceries and $50 in change before the fake bill was discovered. The phoney bill bore the image of President George Bush on the front and had the White House on the back. It also included signs on the front lawn of the White House with slogans such as 'We like broccoli' and 'USA deserves a tax cut'. Instead of being labelled a 'Federal Reserve Note', the fake bill was marked as a 'Moral Reserve Note' and bore the signatures of Ronald Reagan, political mentor; and George HW Bush, campaign adviser and mentor. For the record, the US Mint does not print a $200 bill.

ROLL ALONG NOW!

Bank robbers come in all shapes and sizes, but this one was in a top-of-the-line $5000 sports wheelchair. Ironic because he lost the ability to walk in a botched armed robbery 20 years ago when he robbed a store and the owner got the gun away from him and shot him. Anyway, he was back at it … with another equally ineffective attempt to steal lots of money.

It all started when our wheelchair thief wheeled himself up to the entrance of a bank at 10.00 a.m. one Tuesday morning. When he couldn't get through the security doors at the main entrance, an employee held a side door open for him. Our thief was carrying a small brown paper bag with an ink-scrawled message: 'Robbery—put money in bag' and the number '1500'. Fairly cryptic, but it seems he wanted $1500 in the bag. He first set the note in front of the bank manager, then, realising there was no cash at her desk, gave it to a teller. The teller was decidedly ungenerous and only gave him two $100 notes. When he got to the door, he realised that she had only given him $200 and he went into a blind rage, swearing his head off and throwing down his hold-up note in disgust. He then rolled out the door and headed for the metro, where a security guard stopped him and called police.

FREEZE! THIS IS PLAYSTATION!

A 60-year-old woman was taking care of her three grandsons when four men attempted to burgle her home. The grandchildren happened to be playing a video game called Grand Theft Auto at the time. This is a game where dozens of random police scanner messages blare out calls such as: 'This is the police! Stop, we have you surrounded!' Believe it or not, the burglars heard the soundtrack and thought the police were really outside the house waiting for them. Is this the first time an audio track has single-handedly apprehended four crims?

LULLABY LA LA

A man was robbing a house while the occupants were asleep in bed. He started feeling drowsy as he went from room to room, checking out the goods. When he came to the children's bedroom it was just too tempting, so he climbed to the top of the bunk bed and went to sleep. A little 4-year-old girl woke up in the middle of the night and went in to tell her mother about the 'funny' man in bed. He'll have a couple of years to sleep it off in prison.

FUNNY MONEY

A young male went into a store and purchased $400 worth of merchandise including a DVD player and some DVDs. After he left, an employee noticed the money was fake, but it was too late. They never expected what happened next. About half an hour later, a woman came back into the store with a receipt. She wanted to return $400 worth of goods ... You guessed it, it was the receipt they'd just issued for the bogus money. Clearly, the young lady was planning to return the goods and get real money back, but the store manager made a snap decision and gave her the counterfeit money back again. The manager was stunned to see both the male and female return together about half and hour later to complain that they had been given counterfeit money!

DON'T YOU HAVE ALL-DAY BREAKFAST?

A man attempted to rob a fast food restaurant at 7.50 a.m. one Monday morning. The young lady taking his order said she was sorry, but she couldn't open the cash register without a food order. So the man ordered onion rings. The young lady apologised again. You see, onion rings weren't available for breakfast. Clearly this thief didn't have what it takes ... he walked out in frustration.

JOE WHO?

Two masked gunmen burst into a house and tied up a woman and two of her children with duct tape. They demanded to know where 'Joe' was. When the woman said that she didn't know anyone called Joe and that he certainly didn't live there, the two held a quick discussion and came to the conclusion that they had the wrong house. While they were debating what to do next, one of the woman's children, who hadn't been seen, called police. The men apologised and left the house, only to be greeted by two smiling police officers at the door.

PLAY IT SAM!

Most burglars steal things, some fall asleep on the couch, but not many sit down to play an impromptu Beethoven piano sonata. A police officer was awakened shortly after 2.30 a.m. one morning by the sound of someone breaking through the front door of his house. He grabbed his gun and headed for the living room, where he found an intoxicated 19-year-old man sitting at the piano. The would-be pianist saw the owner come in and got up, but the officer told him to sit back down. It was then that he started playing. Intoxicated as he was, even the police chief had to admit that he played beautifully.

The young man explained to his attentive host that he was looking for a party and had obviously showed up at the wrong place. He wondered if he might get a lift. Certainly, the officer got him a lift—straight to police headquarters.

GREAT GETAWAYS
OF OUR TIME

Why go by car when you can go by tricycle?

Some of the best parts in movies are the chase scenes. Cars roaring down the road, smashing through street stalls and sending fruit and veggies flying, cyclists and pedestrians leaping out of the way. Or in the continental version ... cars weaving their way down quaint narrow cobbled laneways, bumping their way down stairs, scaring the pigeons and ending up in a fountain with a big splash! Cue for audience to laugh uproariously. What a hell of a chase! Well, dumb crook getaways are slightly different. They may involve cars, but then again, they may involve bicycles, steamrollers or lawnmowers. For isn't there a saying: why go by car when you can go by tricycle? Well, if there isn't, there sure ought to be.

LOW-SPEED CHASE

An unhinged 78-year-old man went on a shooting spree at a casino and wounded five people before making his escape. But did he really think he would get away? He was caught as he hobbled towards a fire escape with his walker.

RIDING A WHAT?

Proud of his new purchase, a man went on a joy-ride along the highway. With steering wheel in one hand and beer bottle in the other, his ride ended when he crashed into a parked car which he later told police 'shouldn't have been there'. Nothing new here except that he wasn't driving a car, he was driving his lawnmower!

FULL MARKS FOR NOT GIVING UP!

To avoid a $50 traffic fine, a man sped off, went through a red light, swerved to try and sideswipe the police car off the road, and when he refused to pull over, caused a major police chase operation. Police dropped a strip of spikes onto the road, blowing out his tyres, but he kept going. Finally, as he attempted to do a U-turn across a three-lane highway median strip, he was blocked by a sea of squad cars. Did he give up? No, he made a run for it, but slipped on the median strip and fell over. He was arrested and charged with assault, failure to stop for police, reckless driving, and a few other offences that added up to a possible five years in jail.

WHAT A GETAWAY!

A not-too-bright young man went into a department store, grabbed a VCR, and ran out the fire door. A quick thinking store manager chased him out to the parking lot to get his car registration. The car didn't have plates but it did have a national parks permit with his name and address printed on it. But there's more. As the manager watched, the fellow put his foot to the floor, but the car didn't move. He was out of petrol! So what did he do? Make a run for it? No. Showing a remarkable lack of intelligence, he got out of the car and casually walked across the road to the petrol station, taking the VCR with him. He came back to his car with a petrol tin in one hand and the stolen VCR in the other. He was trying to fill his tank when he felt a tap on his shoulder ...

SPEED 3?

A man walking past a building site decided to steal a steamroller. He led police on a wild five-kilometre chase until an officer managed to clamber on board and stop it.

I'M WITH THEM!

After robbing a bank, a thief without a getaway car ran out into the middle of a busy street to try and lose the police that were chasing him. He couldn't believe his luck when a crowd of joggers appeared around the corner, jogging down the street—the perfect way for him to blend in with the crowd! So, he slipped into the middle of the group and paced himself with them, sure that he could get some distance from the scene with no hassles. What he didn't know was that his group of camouflage runners was actually a bunch of police academy recruits out for a morning run.

BEWARE OF SHARP POINTY THINGS!

Two idiots decided to do a bit of black market trading in deer antlers; they just had to figure out a way to get them out of the national park unseen. There was a ranger checkpoint on leaving the park, so a car wasn't worth the risk. By foot? Well, backpacks could only carry so much, so that wasn't really worth the effort either. How about by boat? Yes, but not quite. After loading their chosen method of transportation to bursting point, they pushed off and began their journey. It was late spring, so the river, which was hazardous at the best of times, now had twice the normal flow of water. They hadn't gone far before they hit some treacherous rapids, and the jiggling antlers punctured their raft. Battling the swirling waters, they were lucky to get to dry land. Next time, why don't you try a hot air balloon, boys?

TOO MUCH TOUR DE FRANCE

Two bank robbers came up with a new kind of getaway vehicle— mountain bikes. The pair hid their bikes around the corner from a bank and then confronted the armoured truck guard who was filling the bank's ATM with cash at about 9.20 a.m. one morning. The guard fought back, pulled out his gun and wounded one of the robbers in the leg. However, they got some cash, ran for their bikes, hopped in the saddle and began shifting gears. After a short, speedy sprint, police caught up with them two blocks away. They hadn't realised that police are well-trained in speed chasing and cutting off suspects in cars, so two bikes—no matter how many gears they have—aren't that much of a challenge.

HEY, THAT'S MY CAR!

A police officer heard a car stereo blaring, came over, and recognised the driver as a man wanted on more than half a dozen warrants. So he asked for some ID, but the driver jumped out of the car and took off. The police officer looked around before quickly deciding his next move: getting into the suspect's car and chasing him! The officer used the car to barricade the wanted man into a nearby café. As he sat watching the place get surrounded by cops, he was probably pondering the concept of the 'getaway car' and wishing he had stayed in his car himself!

ALL ABOARD!

An escaped prisoner flagged down a bus to make his getaway, only to find it was full of police officers looking for him.

TWINKLE TOES

After robbing a motel one night, a crim headed into the woods, sure that the police would never catch him in a million years. Since it was pitch black, the police figured they would never catch him either until one of them noticed something strange—bright red flashing lights in the darkness! To the crim's surprise, police moved in and managed to track him down very easily. Their trick? They just watched his feet—he was wearing novelty flashing shoes that light up when you walk.

SNOW SPEEDSTER

There must be 101 uses for a global positioning satellite network in this crazy mixed-up world ... and here's one of them. Where this story takes place, private snow-removal contractors are required by law to carry a GPS-equipped mobile. This allows the department to effectively schedule ploughing and to verify that the roads are actually being cleared. One snow-removal operator, who probably had been spending too much time alone with the snow, stopped off at a local coffee shop, ordered coffee and flashed the waitress. It was easy to track him down, despite leading police on a tedious low-speed chase.

GETAWAY SHMETAWAY

A couple of would-be bandits robbed a bank at closing time one day and hopped into their getaway car, hoping to make a quick exit from town. They probably should have listened to the traffic report. As they reached the outskirts of town, they found themselves stuck in a huge traffic jam caused by a highway construction project. Total standstill. The two hyped-up crooks were sitting in their stationary car, stewing, when a police officer simply strolled up to them, tapped on the window, and placed them under arrest.

TRIKE HIKE

Police were called to a bizarre crime scene after receiving reports that a man on a tricycle had been seen pedalling down the road, waving a gun around and firing shots. Concentrating on his handgun instead of paying attention to the road, he then slammed into a car, dropping his gun on impact. He picked himself up and demanded to be taken to the hospital, but the driver of the car tried to persuade him that it would be better if they contacted the police. At this point, the tricycle nut opened the rear car door, hopped into the back seat and absolutely insisted that he be taken to the hospital. The driver jumped from the car, screaming for someone to call the police. The tricky tricyclist then got out, mounted his trike ... and toppled over. That's when a police car arrived on the scene, prompting the now tetchy trike rider to abandon his tricycle and hop back into the car—this time with his gun. Officers saw the weapon and ordered him out of the car. Instead he put the car in gear, threw the handgun out the window and took off, failing to notice that the emergency brake was still on. Police then watched as he wove down the street, losing control of the car, and hitting a street sign. He was apprehended moments later, feebly attempting to hide in a nearby lemon tree.

YOU DON'T NEED A GUN

CREATIVE WEAPON IDEAS
FROM ASPIRING THIEVES

Armed robbery generally means stealing something with a gun, right? Well, not having a gun has never stopped some masterminds come up with a whole range of wacky substitute weapons. Some of them are scary; some of them are not. And sometimes the victims of an attempted crime are unsure what to do and even laugh in the face of their assailant. Seriously, what would you do if someone confronted you armed with ... a zucchini? So, for your reading pleasure, here are some creative weapon ideas from aspiring thieves.

DO YOU WANT RICE WITH THAT?

A delivery driver from a Chinese restaurant was jumped on by a group of people with a novel idea of assault—they bashed him over the head with a bag of prawn crackers before stealing his food. When police arrived at the scene of the crime, they noticed a thin tell-tale drizzle of spicy sauce that had leaked from one of the takeaway containers. They followed it to a nearby suspicious-smelling apartment where they arrested three men, a woman, and some prawn crackers.

IT'S A KNOCKOUT!

A man walked into a sandwich shop with his hand in his jacket pocket, announcing that it was a stick-up. In a quick move, a customer behind tapped him on the shoulder and when he turned around, knocked him out with a mean right hook. They held him down until police arrived, when they discovered that his 'gun' was actually a can of chicken noodle soup.

CHAINSAW MASSACRE?

She would've looked pretty scary, but there wasn't a lot of damage she could do ... A 20-year-old woman with a vivid imagination tried a robbery with a difference one night. She entered a motel reception armed with an electric chainsaw ... except it wasn't plugged in!

SAWN-OFF RING FINGER?

A man was arrested for trying to holdup a bank with an innovative assault weapon. He used a thumb and a finger to simulate a gun, but tragically, he forgot to keep his hand in his pocket.

ER, YOU'LL WANT YOUR LOCAL BRANCH

A customer in a bank felt something hard and cold pressed against the small of his back. Then a voice in his ear whispered menacingly, 'This is a robbery!' He knew he was in for it if he didn't hand over the cash he had just withdrawn, so he handed it over. But the other bank customers knew something that our poor victim didn't. As the assailant attempted to flee, they grabbed him, beat him up, and held him until police arrived. Why did the bank customers react so bravely in the face of such danger? Because the would-be robber hadn't used a gun to threaten his victim; he had used a tree branch!

As a police spokesperson said later, 'The authorities are used to dealing with robberies involving guns. But they have never dealt with thieves trying to rob banks with branches before.'

ASSAULTED FISH?

It all started with an argument over a fish burger and ended up with puns galore. A man was up in court ready to plead guilty to a charge of assault. But he baulked at the more serious charge of 'aggravated assault'. The reason? He had attacked his victim with a fish fillet which, when you think about it, does not really seem to be a terribly frightening or fearsome object, does it?

Our fearless defendant had been at a fish and chip shop and didn't like the fish burger he was given and flung the fish fillet back at the shop owner. But when his case was described in court as assault 'with an offensive weapon, namely battered fish', the magistrate questioned the charge and adjourned it for a later date. 'A man holds up a piece of fish and throws it at someone and a fish fillet is an offensive weapon?' he asked. 'What is the world coming to?' Yeah, what!

INTERESTING
VEGETABLES I HAVE KNOWN

A thief got away with a series of 'armed' robberies until the police finally caught up with him. They discovered that through all those years he had been pretending to have a gun under his jacket, he really had a zucchini!

CHOCOLATE OR STRAWBERRY?

An 18-year-old young lady must have been desperate for cash. She attempted to rob a convenience store armed with an ice-cream scoop ... twice! The first time the shopkeeper just stared at her in disbelief, so she lay in wait until the late night shift began and tried the stunt again with a different assistant. This one burst out laughing and asked whether she wanted chocolate or strawberry.

FINGER OF POWER

A masked man stormed into a bank and demanded money, threatening the teller with a gun. The teller said he would get the money and so the robber waited in anticipation, holding his bag open with both hands. Now any fool knows you can't hold a heavy bag of money open and a gun at the same time, so our sharp-witted thief put the gun down on the counter. The teller seized her chance, grabbed the gun, and suddenly the tables had turned. The confused robber raised his arm and, forgetting that his gun was missing, menaced the teller with his index finger. Realising that his situation was not as strong as he had anticipated, he fled the bank on an old bike that broke down at the end of the street.

THE POWER OF POSITIVE THINKING

Police called in a man to explain how his bank account had grown from $200 to $4 million dollars within a week. The man explained that he had made a number of deposits by inserting empty envelopes into the bank's ATM. And then—this is the truly amazing part—by meditating on the empty envelopes and using the power of 'positive thinking' he was able to magically transform his $200 account into a multi-million dollar stash. Wow! Despite all the positive thinking in the world, police weren't convinced.

WHAT A HAM!

Three teenagers went into a corner store and asked for some sliced ham. The shopkeeper went out the back and when he returned, the two of them jumped him. 'They hit me in the head with something,' he said. 'It hurt like the dickens, but I didn't go down.' What the teens didn't know was that the shopkeeper was an amateur boxer. He was in no mood to give up his hard-earned money to some bratty kids. And, what's more, he was holding a potential weapon in his hands— a two-kilogram hunk of ham! The shopkeeper lunged at them with the ham and according to his statement 'got one real good in the stomach with a left'. The teens fled from the shop pursued by a furious shopkeeper wildly waving a giant ham!

DANGEROUS HAIR CARE WEAPON

An interesting looking guy with a handbag went into a 24-hour supermarket about 4.30 a.m. He walked round and round for about 15 minutes with the bag open, peering at this and that, so that the two employees kept an eye on him for possible shoplifting. Finally one of the employees asked if he needed any help. He didn't, but said he needed to go to the bathroom. He went in, then came out again fairly rapidly, without his bag. One of the employees snuck into the bathroom while the guy was at the front of the store and found a curling wand and a towel on the counter. Not too long after, the guy went back into the bathroom. The co-workers decided he was acting too weird, so they called the company's security. While one of them was on the phone to security, the guy suddenly burst out of the bathroom with a woman's singlet on his face and what looked like a gun ... it turned out to be the curling wand! He politely demanded that they put their hands up and hand over all the money, lottery tickets and cigarettes, which they did. While this was going on, two innocent customers walked in, and police were moving into position around the store, but the weird guy didn't seem to notice. He warned his victims not to move or call the police for five minutes, then he went out into the night, only to be greeted by the sounds of police yelling, 'Freeze! Get down on the ground!' He stood there dazed before turning round and going back into the store. He carefully put everything on the counter—the stolen goods, the towel, even his curling wand. Without a word, he made a dignified turn on the spot and went outside to meet his fate with a great opening line, 'Hey guys, what's going on? I'm not doing anything.'

THIS IS A CHOC-UP!

A man tried to rob a convenience store with a chocolate bar, but for some strange reason, the shop assistant and customers began to laugh. Miffed, he ran away.

SUPER FINGER!

A masked man tried to rob a pharmacy one Sunday night 'armed' only with his fingers. The would-be robber didn't even try to conceal his pointed finger in a pocket to fool anybody into thinking he was holding a gun. He simply held up his gloved hand and pointed his finger, with his thumb extended like the cocked hammer of a pistol. It didn't work.

At first, the pharmacist didn't believe he was being robbed. He chuckled and asked whether it was a robbery. 'Yeah, this is a robbery,' replied the masked marvel before giving him a nudge with his 'gun' finger. The pharmacist wrestled the intruder down a flight of stairs. During the fracas, he managed to pull off the makeshift mask and recognised the assailant—he had recently been accused of forging prescriptions at the pharmacy. And so our masked friend was charged with attempted robbery, but not attempted armed robbery, since a finger isn't a weapon—even if some dumb crooks think it is!

HAVE FINGER, WILL USE IT!

Late one night, a masked bandit burst into a service station, aimed his index finger at the attendant, and demanded money. 'You've got to be kidding,' said the attendant. The man moved in closer. The attendant grabbed the masked marvel's finger and twisted it as hard as he could. Screaming in pain, the bandit made a quick exit.

MY ASSAULT WEAPON IS ALIVE!

Why did he do it? A man is facing battery charges after he swung a metre-long alligator at his girlfriend during an argument. Why it was in his bathtub in the first place is an even greater mystery.

I'M ARMED AND DANGEROUS ... AND DESPERATE

A man broke into a fast food outlet early one morning and was found by police trying to open a safe with a spatula.

DOPES WITH DOPE

How to get caught with illegal substances!

Here are a few gems about those intellectual giants who get involved in the drug world. At the best of times, most thieves aren't that good at thinking things through, but after they've smoked a few joints, it's amazing how muddled their thinking can become. They say and do the most stupid things ... usually when there are police around. If anything, these stories illustrate just how easy it is to get caught!

THEY DON'T CALL IT CRACK FOR NOTHING

A car was pulled over by police for failing to stop at a stop sign. As it happens, the passenger had a warrant out for drug trafficking and was arrested. At the jail, it was discovered he was carrying crack in a bag, only due to the vigilance of a young officer who noticed that when the crim bent over to put on his jail uniform, he had a plastic bag sticking out of his behind!

JUST THIS MARIJUANA, OFFICER

A man was pulled over when an officer spotted him driving with a cracked windscreen. He was arrested when a check revealed that the car was not licensed or registered. Police then asked whether he would like to take anything from his car before being taken to the station to be booked. The man took a child's car seat from the back of his car and then, to the officer's amazement, opened the boot and took out a small plastic bag with a strong smell of marijuana. Turns out it had a street value of $6000 and the man was booked for more than just driving offences.

SOMEONE STOLE OUR GRASS!

You can't get much more brainless than this. An 18-year-old male and his 17-year-old girlfriend went to police to report that their stash of marijuana had been stolen from their apartment. They explained to a very interested official that they needed it back because they planned to sell it. When the deputies arrived, the couple allowed them to search the apartment where they found several marijuana plants.

WHAT A HEADACHE!

One night, two undercover police officers were in the driveway of an alleged drug dealer, waiting for her to come home. A young man arrived, wanting to see the same person. They got into a conversation with the guy who assured them he could get cocaine from his dealer. He made a call and they all agreed to meet a few streets away. True to his word, the guy showed up with the goods and, as expected, wanted some as payment for his troubles. Obviously police aren't allowed to hand over cocaine to any old bloke on the street, so the guy watched with great expectation as the officer held the bag of cocaine over the cellophane from a cigarette pack and began dropping headache powder from the palm of his hand. The unsuspecting guy could not believe how generous his new 'friend' was. After thanking them many times, they parted ways.

Later, the police stopped by their new 'friend's' house and arrested him for the sale and delivery of cocaine. He didn't think he should be charged because the stuff they'd given him was so lousy!

QUE SERA SERA

A British man who smuggled more than 9000 ecstasy tablets past Bangkok customs was later arrested in a park for not wearing a shirt!

THIS ONE'S A BIT HARD TO SWALLOW

Doctors see some interesting cases, but this one takes the cake. A man walked into a doctor's surgery with a coathanger stuck down his throat. He claimed that he was using it as a hook to fish a cocaine-filled balloon from down his throat. And how did the balloon of cocaine get down there? The man said he was at a party Monday night when someone slipped a balloon full of cocaine into his drink. Police found this hard to swallow.

FOLLOW YOUR NOSE

There are some things that the best air freshener in the world just can't cover up, as one dope dealer discovered. Police were searching an apartment building for a suspect wanted on 10 warrants ranging from distribution of cocaine to assault, when they were distracted by a very heady aroma coming from an upstairs window. Once they'd applied for a search warrant, they went in and were struck by the smell of marijuana, which the occupant had attempted to conceal with air fresheners. Indeed, police found an astonishing number of household cleaners—deodorisers, air fresheners and window cleaners—but the smell of weed was just too strong. They also found what they suspected—a $200 000 stash of marijuana which the 30-year-old occupant had lamely attempted to conceal by covering it with a rug!

I'M FLYING ... BUT NOT IN A PLANE!

Colleagues noticed a certain airline pilot was under a lot of stress. Well, he finally cracked. He was sentenced to four months in jail after being convicted of jamming the air traffic control frequency and jeopardising airport safety for 20 minutes. How did he manage that? By singing: 'Flintstones, meet the Flintstones ... ' over and over again on the radio while landing his plane.

PASTRY PIZZAZZ!

What do police do with confiscated drugs? Of course, they act professionally and ethically and dispose of the alleged illegal substances. Well, one bunch of zany drug squad members decided to play a little prank. On a weekend team building exercise, they brought along homemade pastries ... and mixed up in the dough was 400 grams of hashish. Then they served them out and sat back to watch the fun. Well, it wasn't that much fun. The chief of the drug squad collapsed unconscious and 11 other members suffered nausea and fainting attacks. The pranksters received suspended jail sentences ... Hey guys, can't you take a little joke!

BATTLE OF THE BULGE

A man in court on charges of drug possession argued that the charges shouldn't stand because he had been searched without a warrant. The prosecutor said the officer didn't need a warrant because a 'bulge' in his jacket could have been a gun. 'Nonsense,' said the man, who happened to be wearing the same jacket that he had been arrested in. To prove his point, he made a great show of removing his jacket and handing it over so the judge could investigate. The judge reached inside the jacket pocket ... and pulled out a packet of cocaine. The judge was laughing so hard that the hearing had to be adjourned for five minutes so he could compose himself.

WHAT'S THIS TANKER DOING HERE?

Two dealers had a methamphetamine lab set up in their house. One of the primary ingredients in the manufacture of meth is anhydrous ammonia, which usually comes in relatively small canisters. But our lab rats must have had their sights set on greater things; they managed to car-jack, or should we say 'truck-jack', a 9600-gallon tanker of ammonia—the type that is hauled around by hulking great 18 wheelers. They parked it right in front of their house, with a hose running from the tank to the front door. Needless to say, it was not the most unobtrusive house in the street. And indeed it attracted the interest of several law enforcement agencies ...

SPACED-OUT

Police took a call from a spaced-out individual who reported that his house had been broken into. When the police arrived, our not-quite-all-there young friend directed them to the closet where he was positive the robber was hiding. The cops took a look inside—definitely no burglar—but there were a couple of marijuana plants that our friend had to admit belonged to him.

TRUST ME, I REALLY AM STUPID!

For a dare, a 27-year-old man walked up to police at 1.00 a.m. on a Tuesday morning and told them he wanted to be arrested 'for being stupid'. When police told him that wasn't a crime, he invited them back to his apartment where they found marijuana and drug paraphernalia. He proved his point.

BE NICE TO PEOPLE WHO SERVE FOOD

A young woman was working at the drive-through window for a fast food restaurant. A car pulled up full of obnoxious teens, drinking, smoking dope, and high on other things too. There were seven of them and after handing over their money, they started harassing the woman. When the driver had the nerve to blow smoke in her face, she'd had enough. She told them to pull into an empty parking space to wait for their food. They did as she asked and, while they were waiting, she called the police. Within minutes, a swarm of patrol cars pulled into the parking lot. Mission accomplished, but there's more. While they were being arrested, the driver received a text message that read 'I've got the merchandise, meet me at ...' The police met the sender of the text message and the next day came back to the takeaway joint, shook the young woman's hand, and told her that she'd helped them with one of the biggest drug busts they'd ever had.

BIRDIE? WELL, THAT'S A
LITTLE FEATHERED FRIEND

An overseas tourist on a golf holiday came through customs, golf bag in tow. One of the customs officials noticed that he seemed a little on edge and couldn't stop chattering to other airline passengers in the queue. While making idle conversation about golf, the official realised that the tourist didn't have a clue about the game—he didn't even know what a 'handicap' was. So he asked his chatty companion to demonstrate his swing, which he did—backwards! Needless to say, the golf bag was examined carefully and a substantial amount of narcotics was found.

IT'S NOT MINE!

To get into a courthouse, you have to walk through a metal detector. One man set off the alarm as he walked through, so he was told to empty his pockets. As he was emptying his jacket, he pulled out four rocks of crack. He looked at them, swallowed hard, and said the drugs weren't his. The officer questioned that, wondering why it came from his coat. 'It's someone else's coat,' the man explained.

HOW DID THAT GET THERE?

A police officer stopped a car for a minor traffic infringement. It turned out to be Mr X, a local drug dealer and thug, well known to police. The man was only too happy to hand over his driver's licence and follow procedures to get a ticket. The police officer then asked if he had any guns or drugs in the car. Mr X was terribly indignant and launched into a five-minute tirade about being an honest working citizen and that there was no reason for him to be harassed and how dare the police do this and do that ... Then he pulled three wads of cash from his pocket in a flamboyant manner just to prove how hard-working he really was. Problem was he also pulled out a plastic bag full of cocaine.

WHERE WERE YOU
ON THE NIGHT OF ... ?

When questioned about a recent bank robbery, a not-so-smart crook had the most brilliant of alibis—he was in another state buying heroin at the time. Not only that, he had the hotel receipt to prove it! Police went to the hotel, searched the room, and found 84 packets of heroin. The man was, naturally enough, charged with several offences, just not that particular robbery.

SAY, AREN'T YOU THE POLICE?

Narcotics officers were cruising slowly along on a routine patrol when a 17-year-old student—who should have been at school at the time—waved them down. The young man opened the back door of the police car, jumped in, and asked the officers what they wanted and how much. He then directed them to a side street, saying the area was 'too hot'. The officers asked for 'two pieces'—that is two pieces of crack. The young man then gave the two officers a funny look and said, 'You know, you guys look like cops,' The driver smiled. 'Maybe that's because we're wearing police raid jackets with the word 'POLICE' in big black letters on the sleeves and the back and the front,' he said.

GULP!

Cruising police spotted a long-time member of a well-known gang sitting in a parked car in a car park. The officers stopped and searched the vehicle and discovered a plastic bag, which they suspected was full of drugs. As the gang member was being questioned, he suddenly grabbed the plastic bag and began to scuffle with police. He put up a good fight but was eventually subdued with pepper spray. While one police officer kept him restrained, the other began to search for the plastic bag. It was nowhere to be seen. Before long, police noticed that the gang member became strangely subdued. He turned white as a sheet, stopped talking, and finally stopped breathing. The police officers began resuscitation and discovered that he had swallowed the plastic bag. They found it stuck an impressively long way down his throat and managed to extract it with a pair of pliers. The man revived, only to be jailed on drug and assault charges.

UN-AWARE

Imagine you're a drug dealer and you're standing on the street selling drugs to a buyer. Then, let's say, two police cars arrive at a nearby residence with lights flashing and sirens wailing. Wouldn't you put your transaction on 'hold' for a little while and maybe scoot? That didn't occur to one young dealer who was in the middle of a drug deal with a wired informant when two police cars responding to a domestic incident arrived on the scene. Two police officers listening to the wired conversation in a nearby unmarked car thought the gig was up. Surely, they thought, the deal would fall through once police cars arrived with sirens and flashing lights. But no. With all the hubbub happening just metres away, the guy kept going with the deal. They heard every word and were able to arrest him.

I WANT MY MONEY BACK

Police were intrigued when a man walked into his local police station with a large bag of cocaine. He dropped it on the counter, informed the officer on duty that it was substandard, and asked that the person who sold it to him be arrested immediately.

SOMETHING IN THE AIR

Early one morning police responded to a burglar alarm at a private residence. While making sure there was no break-in, the responding officer was greeted by the distinct aroma of marijuana. The owners of the residence were nowhere to be found so the officer drove away, got a warrant, came back, and discovered 2475 marijuana plants ... a dope growing operation worth an estimated $4 million. The moral of the story is: if you're doing something illegal in the privacy of your own home, make sure your burglar alarm doesn't go off!

OUCH!

*Self-inflicted wounds and daring
physical feats all in the name of crime ...*

A life of crime might mean diamonds and luxury yachts, beautiful companions, champagne, caviar and never having to work again. But then again, it may mean fracturing your skull, breaking your nose, or knocking yourself out through sheer greed and stupidity. You'll be amazed at the things would-be crims do to get what they want. Gasp at their bravado and have a good laugh at their outrageous capacity to inflict severe physical pain on themselves.

YEOWEEE!

An 80-year-old woman was awoken by a crashing sound in her bathroom. She went to investigate and found a burglar in a rather awkward position. He was dangling from her window and had impaled his testicles on the broken shards of glass. The man cried out, 'I'm dying'; the old woman cried back, 'Good!' She alerted neighbours who called the police and an ambulance. The man lost a lot of self-confidence, two litres of blood, and half of a very vital organ.

GOT HIM ON THE REBOUND!

A thief was feeling pretty pleased with himself. He was on a roll and had gotten away with three crimes in a row. His modus operandi was always the same—he would throw bricks through a jewellery store window and make off with the loot. The fourth time round he didn't get away. After throwing a brick into a plexiglass window, the brick bounced back, hit him in the head, and knocked him out cold until the police arrived.

AN INANIMATE OBJECT
KNOCKED ME OUT!

A man who'd had a bit too much to drink was discovered by police fast asleep on a railway line ... not the safest place in the world for a kip. He couldn't remember how he had gotten there, but he did recall that he had been knocked out cold. Believing that he had been attacked, the police asked him whether he could remember anything about his mystery assailant. Yes, as a matter of fact he could. He explained that he had been asleep when something woke him—a 15-car coal train. 'I sat up,' he said 'and it knocked me out.'

RIP

A dumb crook was cleaning a shotgun that had not been firing properly. He used a cigarette lighter to check the gunpowder in the barrel when ... well, you know the rest and it ain't pretty.

TIM-BERRRRR!

Two teens came up with a very stupid way to get some free lengths of aluminium, which they were then going to sell for scrap metal. After dark, they set to work with wrenches to take apart an electrical tower. But rather awkwardly, the tower decided to collapse on top of them. You see, they actually started at the bottom and were disassembling the supports, rather than starting at the top, which most people would see as the better option. One of them was crushed severely; the other managed to dig himself out from under the rubble. As dumb crooks go, they rank pretty highly.

SCARRED FOR LIFE

A hospital isn't a prime target for most thieves, after all, what exactly is there to steal? And what could possible make it worth your while? Well, this thief found out the hard way. After evading security staff and helping himself to a doctor's coat and paging device, a thief with time on his hands spotted a sunbed. Seeing the perfect opportunity to get a tan, he removed his clothes for a 45-minute session. However, the high-voltage UV machine at the hospital is used to treat burns victims and has a maximum dosage of 10 seconds. After lying on the bed for almost 300 times the recommended maximum time, the man was covered in blisters. Hours later, when the pain became unbearable, he went to another hospital about 30 kilometres away. Staff became suspicious because he was wearing a doctor's coat and his story about how he got the burns just didn't add up. They were kind enough to tend his wounds before calling the police.

JUST GIVE YOURSELF UP!

When flashers do their thing, they probably don't expect a wild goose chase, but that's exactly what happened to one brainless man who exposed himself to a woman sitting at a bus stop. He happened to time it very poorly—two officers on patrol saw him 'flash'. So off he ran, leading them on a low-speed chase through the city streets for 20 minutes, pelting them with fruit several times (but missing) and then climbing a shop awning and threatening to kill himself. Police tried to talk him down but that didn't work so they shot him with 10 rounds of plastic bullets. Did that stop him? No. He finally surrendered after being sprayed for five minutes with a high-powered water hose. And for the pièce de résistance, as he began to climb down the awning, he accidentally knocked himself out on one of the metal supports.

WHAT A WAY TO GO!

A 28-year-old jail escapee managed to elude police by jumping into a river and attempting to swim to the other side. Wouldn't you know it, he was eaten by a crocodile.

YOU ONLY HAVE TO ASK ...

A bird-brained man decided to steal the engine of an old Bedford tip truck for purposes unknown. Now, with an engine that size, it takes about three good-sized men to lift it, but our daredevil dude decided to go solo and remove the engine from below, rather than the conventional out-the-top-with-a-crane technique. So, he crawled under the chassis, began to loosen the bolts ... and the engine fell on top of him. The last words of this sorry tale go to the manager of the truck company who explained to police that the truck was about to be taken away for scrap: 'If he had come and asked for it, I would have given it to him.'

SOMEWHERE ON
THE COAST OF AFRICA ...

A retired colonel who seems to have gone gaga in his old age bought a 'magic' belt that would supposedly protect him from bullets—well, he was a highly superstitious fellow. The colonel had the son of the belt maker fire several bullets at him to test the belt. Did it work? No. He died instantly and the unwilling assassin is still on the run, not too keen to bump into any of the colonel's bodyguards.

RIDE 'EM COWBOY!

One night, a police officer went to investigate reports of an inebriated man standing naked in his front yard shooting at random cars. As the officer's car pulled up, the man took a pot shot at him. The officer got out of his car and walked towards the naked man who, in an ingenious attempt to escape, jumped onto the back of his German shepherd. Oddly enough, the dog didn't appreciate this. Instead of taking off like a thoroughbred, it turned on his owner and attacked him.

YEOW-EEE!

A bright spark decided to rob a bank—a blood bank. No vampire jokes, please. He cased the joint and figured that by breaking in on Friday night he would have all the time in the world because the place didn't open up again until 8 o'clock on Monday morning.

It seemed to him that the most obvious way to gain entry was to climb down an airshaft from the roof. His operation began at 10.00 p.m. on Friday night and was going as planned until he lost his grip and slipped down an eight-metre vertical shaft. He came to an awkward and abrupt stop in the office, well, actually not quite *in* the office, more like dangling *over* the office. He came to a halt a metre above an office partition, with one leg hanging on either side. He simply couldn't budge, not up or down, no matter how hard he tried. Unable to move, he remained in this uncomfortable suspended state until Monday morning when he was discovered suffering from dehydration and delirious from pain. You would be too if your testicles were swollen to the size of grapefruits—each one that is! After lowering him down to freedom, the owners didn't press charges. Rightly or wrongly, they felt that he had suffered enough.

DISAPPEARING ROPE TRICK

Late one Thursday night, a man robbed a large department store by cutting a hole in the roof and lowering himself down with a rope. Once inside, he pulled down the rope and helped himself to everything he could lay his eyes on. It was only after he had the haul ready to go, that he realised he couldn't get out the way he came in. So he went off to the garden section and scored himself a ladder. Even though it was a little too short for his needs, he climbed up anyway, slipped and fell. When the store opened on Friday morning, store personnel were intrigued to find a man lying on his back with a broken leg and a ladder by his side. And a visit to hospital was closely followed by a visit to jail.

MAN BITES DOG

Yes, apparently this really happened ... in Edinburgh of all places! Becoming a tad too impatient with his overly enthusiastic guide dog, a blind man dragged it across a busy road and bit it on the head. He now faces charges of animal cruelty.

NICE OF YOU TO DROP IN!

The golden rule before any burglary is to always case the joint; this may prevent any unnecessary embarrassment. Well, this particular burglar paid no heed to this. From a side alley, he climbed onto the roof of a convenience store intending to go in, get the goods, and escape before daylight. He cut a hole to get through the roof but botched the job and ended up falling through the ceiling onto the self-serve coffee machine. Two problems: one, the man had not realised that the store was open 24 hours a day; and two, who was standing at the machine about to make himself a cup of coffee? A friendly police officer with time on his hands.

SNOW STUPIDITY

For a lark, three young men decided to hit the slopes at a ski resort at 3.00 a.m. one Wednesday morning. Not having any toboggans, they stole some yellow foam from the base of one of the legs of the ski lift tower and made a makeshift sled. Two of the men had a great sled ride; the third didn't make it. He crashed into the base of the ski lift tower and died ... And yes, the one that did him in was the one that no longer had the foam cushion to protect skiers because it had been STOLEN!

NOT LONG ENOUGH!

A would-be jail escapee tied eight bed sheets together and climbed out of his seventh-floor window, only to find that the rope finished 10 metres above the ground. Rather than being caught 'hanging around', he jumped. He is now in the jail hospital with a fractured ankle.

WHAT GOES AROUND COMES AROUND

A middle-aged man sat quietly through the Sunday morning service at a local church. When the offering basket was passed around, fellow worshippers were taken aback to see him stashing handfuls of the money into his pockets. Realising he had been spotted, he dashed out of the church and onto a busy road where he was hit by a bus.

SPIKED!

Where this story takes place are a lot of exotic cacti, some reaching up to a very impressive 10 metres high. It used to be popular pastime to use them for practising marksmanship, but it is now illegal. Cacti shooters risk a $100 000 fine and three years in prison, but that didn't stop one sharpshooter who opened fire on a nine-metre cactus with a 16-gauge shotgun. He didn't get to the 'Tim-berrrr ...' bit; he only got to the first syllable before the hulking great plant fell on top of him, crushing him in a rather nasty fashion.

EXPLOSION!

Hey, let's steal some fireworks and blow ourselves up! That's virtually what two young men did when they chose a rather dubious way to light a large quantity of black market fireworks they had stolen. They connected their detonation fuses to a motorcycle battery and then started the engine. The resulting explosion could be heard two kilometres away. Eight onlookers were treated for injuries and the two men came to an unpleasant end and will steal no more.

NO SMOKING

A teenage boy at an airport snuck off to have a smoke. He was puffing away when he saw security guards coming towards him. Not wanting to get caught smoking in a no smoking zone, he shoved the still smouldering cigarette into his shirt pocket. Of course, that's where he had a box of matches. The matches ignited and soon he was hollering for help, clothing ablaze, feeling like a real idiot.

SNEAKY SNAKEY

A teenage boy who loved snakes wanted to start a collection, so in a clear leap of logic, he decided the best way to do this was to break into the zoo and steal two Gabon vipers. This kind of snake is quite sedentary—which is good—but it is also one of the most venomous snakes in the world—which is bad. The snakes behaved themselves until the boy put them in a garbage bag and got onto a bus. In the confines of the bus, the snakes started warming up and didn't like it one bit. That's when they tried to escape from their uncomfortable makeshift home. Trying to keep the snakes happy while concealing them from the other passengers proved too much. The boy was bitten and rushed to hospital. He was given anti-venom serum and luckily for him, regained consciousness. But he never got those snakes home.

I'M LOADED AND SO IS MY GUN!

A man went home to get a shotgun after getting into an argument in a pub. As he was coming back, he accidentally fired it into his testicles! In severe pain, he abandoned the gun in a rubbish bin and crawled back home (very carefully!). Later, he told officers that he was so drunk he had no idea why he went to fetch the weapon or how he had managed to shoot himself. But being in possession of a banned gun got him into lots of trouble. At his court appearance, the magistrate observed that 'shooting yourself' is plainly an exceptional circumstance but she wouldn't reduce the sentence—five years in jail!

I'M HUNGRY, OFFICER!

After she was put into custody for forgery, a woman grabbed her phoney $4125 cheque and ate it. She also tried to eat her fake ID, but police grabbed it before she could. So what does she get apart from a stomach-ache? Charges of felony, identity fraud, obstruction of a police officer ... and an extra charge of tampering with evidence.

JUST DROPPIN' IN!

A crim who'd just served five years for burglary got out of jail and within 12 hours decided to rob a café. He dropped into the building through a grease vent in the roof. His problem was that he had miscalculated his height in relation to the length of the vent. When he kicked the plate off the bottom of the vent, his feet only just stuck through the ceiling. This meant that he had to make a jump ... not knowing what was beneath him or how far he had to fall. As he slipped down, he gashed his hand badly on a broken piece of the metal vent. Bleeding badly, he landed on a stainless steel countertop below. It just happened that the counter was rather greasy. As the crim's rubber-soled joggers landed, he slipped off the counter, crashed onto the tile floor and knocked himself unconscious. Four hours later he came to, covered in blood with a badly cut hand and a broken nose. Wisely deciding to abort the robbery, he figured the best escape route was via the front door ... exactly the same time as a security guard walked by on his regular patrol.

NOT A GOOD NIGHT

A would-be thief experienced what can only be described as a total stuff-up in his first break and enter offence. The random home he selected happened to be owned by a police officer, who freaked him out the moment he climbed in the window by firing a gun (and missing). Scared out of his wits and realising he was in trouble, the burglar attempted to flee the scene, but only succeeded in stumbling painfully into a bed of cactus prettily arranged as a window display. After freeing himself from the prickly plants and losing his knife in the process, he scrambled over the garden fence—a decorative wrought-iron fence—that speared him in the groin. As he was led away, he was heard to mutter, 'Not a good night.'

IT'S A BOY? IT'S A GIRL? IT'S A GUN!

A female prisoner tried to smuggle an automatic pistol into a high-security prison by—er, how do we say this?—shoving it up her rectum. But when she came to remove it, she couldn't do it. In great distress and needing medical attention, she told the wardens that she was pregnant and was rushed to a nearby hospital. After three days of hospitalisation, she confessed the real reason for her pain to hospital staff and the 7.65-kilogram pistol was surgically removed ... ouch!

THAT TAKES BALLS

Two youths broke into an apartment, held-up a man at gunpoint and fled. Officers responding to the robbery found one of them lying on the ground in a nearby car park, clutching his genitals and screaming in agony. He told police he had been shot during the robbery, and the bullet had gone through his underwear and into his leg. No bullet holes were found in his pants to support the claim that he'd been shot by someone else. But the man insisted that he had been shot ... until much later. Finally he sheepishly admitted that he had stuffed a gun down his pants prior to the robbery. The gun went off during the get-away ... and he shot himself in the balls.

I'LL PUNCH MY LIGHTS OUT!

After gambling and losing heaps of money at a well-known casino, a man roughed himself up in the car park and then called police to report that he had been robbed. He smashed his head against a light pole, smudged dirt on his cheeks and, after checking the damage in his car mirror, repeated the process until he achieved just the right 'I-have-been-attacked' look. A good story, but not quite good enough ... surveillance cameras recorded everything.

STINKY STORY

Police chasing a suspected shoplifter into the woods thought they were losing him ... that is until a skunk sprayed the suspect in the face. It didn't stop him but it did slow him down enough for police to catch him. The smelly suspect was taken to the police station and their new star recruit was christened 'Officer Pepé Le Pew'.

WHY IS MY SKIN BRIGHT RED?

A thief went to a lot of trouble to get into a weather station. He managed to get through three barbed wire fences and climb a 40-metre spiral staircase. And what did he get for his trouble? A measly $300 worth of electrical tools and a potentially damaging dose of radiation. Human exposure to the Doppler radar dome that was on the roof of the weather station can result in permanent damage to soft tissue—in other words, your eyes and your testicles. If you're still out there, thief, see your doctor!

STICK IT IN THE FREEZER!

A cashier spotted a man behaving strangely in the checkout queue. He was hopping around, swaying erratically, and scratching his groin. She called a security officer and the man immediately confessed that he had stuffed a frozen chicken drumstick down his pants!

I'LL JUST RUN OVER MYSELF

A 17-year-old youth taking a pick-up truck for a joy-ride caught the attention of police when he began to weave in and out of traffic dangerously. When confronted by police, he jumped from the truck and tried to make a run for it. The truck began to roll, the driver ducked in front of it, fell over, and got run over. Happily he was hospitalised with only minor injuries ... and next time he'll remember to use the handbrake.

ITCHY AND SCRATCHY?

A robbery suspect hiding out at a friend's place got word that a police officer was headed for the front door. So he jumped out a side window stark naked and landed straight in a bush of poison ivy.

YOU CAN LET GO NOW!

A pair of crooks broke into a timber yard. They tried to steal a table saw that was still packed in the shipping box and weighed over 20 kilograms. One of the crooks climbed up in the loft where it was stored, grabbed hold of it, and then hoisted it over a wooden rail. The problem? He forgot to let go of the box. As it was rather heavy, he plunged over the rail, landing on his head and causing severe injuries. He got concussion too, but his partner in crime didn't and police were pleased to hear his side of the story.

MIND THE DROP!

A man coolly sauntered into the front doors of a hotel and drew out a handgun, ready to commit an armed robbery. Police were called and arrived within seconds. As they burst through the front doors, the robber ran to the back of the hotel and climbed out a window to get away. Unfortunately for him, the hotel was built on a steep slope and the rear window was 10 metres above the ground. You can guess the rest ... with a fractured pelvis and broken leg among other injuries, he didn't get too far. In fact, police were thoughtful enough to set up a special court in his hospital ward two days later where—surprise, surprise!—he pleaded guilty.

SHORRY, JUSH
SHSMASHED INTO THE DOOR!

It was 9.00 p.m. and an electrical store had just closed for the evening. Standard procedure was for one of the retail managers to go over and lock the front door so that they could finish business with those who were still in the store while no one else could come in.

There were two young boys about 13 or 14 years old hanging around who had been in the store for over half an hour. They were working their way down an aisle along one wall, piling a few goods up along the way, like they were going to purchase them. When they got to within about four metres of the front door, the boy with all the goods in his arms made a run for it, only to realise the hard way that the door was locked. He ran smack bang into it, the goods flew up in the air, and he landed on his back with a thump.

The manager dialled the boy's home number and spoke to his long-suffering father, explaining the situation. His father asked if they had called the police and when told they hadn't, he exclaimed, 'Well, you should have!'

SELF-SERVICE

A 20-year-old man told police he was wounded in a drive-by shooting while using a pay phone. But after several hours of questioning, he confessed that it wasn't quite like that. He was a gang member and had reached for his gun when he saw rival members approaching. But the gun went off when he tried to draw it from his waistband and he shot himself in the buttocks! It wasn't his lucky night ... police searched his car and found the gun, another gun that turned out to be stolen, and methamphetamine.

THE AMAZING ALCOHOL MAN!

A man staggering across a road was hit by an oncoming car. In an incident like this, the driver is tested for drink driving but in this case it was clearly the pedestrian who had been having a heavy drinking session. Incredulous doctors carried out five blood tests on the man to confirm his blood alcohol reading because they simply could not believe it. A 0.55 blood-alcohol level is usually considered life-threatening but this man, a healthy 67-year-old, had a blood-alcohol level of 0.914—far above the life-threatening range.

Police officers thought the result was inaccurate because the man was conscious and talking to them, but laboratory tests of five subsequent blood samples taken the same day confirmed the initial reading—0.914 blood-alcohol content. It should be illegal to walk with a reading like that.

WHACK ON THE HEAD

Timing is all-important in the wonderful world of crooks. Walking down the street one sunny morning, a would-be car thief saw the car of his dreams and decided to go for it. As it happens, the driver had just parked and was occupied attaching her anti-theft device to the steering wheel. Without much forward planning, the robber decided to make his move. As he came towards her, the woman reacted immediately and smashed him over the head with her crook lock ... yeow!

WHAT A LIVE WIRE!

Why anyone would want to steal copper cable is a mystery, but if you're going to do it, make sure it doesn't have 12 000 volts of electricity running through it. Seems obvious, doesn't it? But one man was badly burnt and knocked out power to 1600 homes and businesses for over five hours when he attempted the impossible. Being breathlessly stupid, the man crawled through a tunnel to an underground junction box where he attempted to cut through a 12 000-volt distribution line. The guy started to cut through the cable, but he didn't get all the way through. He only managed to break through the outer layer of insulation, and that's when he was electrocuted. Shocked, physically and emotionally.

In a dazed state, he crawled to a service station where he looked a sight. Police were called to attend to the poor suffering fool who smelled of burnt hair and skin and who was severely burnt on his upper torso. Lucky to be alive, really.

ALL IN A DAY'S JOG

A man in jogging gear came running into a supermarket at a smart pace. He jogged around the store grabbing bread rolls, cheese, a bottle of wine and several other picnic items. Without breaking pace, he jogged down an unopened checkout lane and out the door. With the manager, two packers, and a checkout assistant in pursuit, the jogger crossed the street, looked back over his shoulder smugly and taunted them with a cheeky, 'You'll never catch me!' Then he ran slap-bang into a telegraph pole and fractured his right cheekbone.

PERRY MASON, EAT YOUR HEART OUT!

Courtroom scenes to make you cringe!

Did you hear the one about the young offender who came to his court hearing dressed in a T-shirt with 'PSYCHO' splashed across the front? His parole officer was horrified and told him to turn his T-shirt back-to-front. He did and entered court, chest emblazoned with the word 'KILLER'.

Well, maybe that's not a true crime story, but it helps not to get the judge and jury offside. That's why you have slithery velvet-tongued barristers smooth-talking their way out of anything they can — sometimes succeeding, sometimes not. And that's why some dumb crooks get so nervous and blurt out things they later regret. Court can be a pretty intimidating place, especially if you're a young first-time crook with a guilty conscience to begin with. So sit back and enjoy some real courtroom clangers!

DON'T ASK QUESTIONS

A man was up in court on a charge of robbing a school. During proceedings, he happened to ask why some schools had alarms and the judge asked him why he wanted to know. 'Cause the one I robbed did,' he replied before realising that he had just put his foot firmly in his mouth. The result? Five years for break and enter.

TOO MUCH INFORMATION

Three men charged with escaping from jail were due to appear in court. One wanted to be tried separately, claiming that he wasn't involved with the escape of the other two. He was granted permission and decided to represent himself. In front of the whole court, he stood up with confidence and said, 'I didn't escape with them. I escaped two hours later down the elevator shaft.'

WHERE ARE MY FLOATIES?

One morning in court, a prisoner waiting for his case to come up decided to make good his escape. He successfully ran out of the courthouse and down the main street towards the town dock where he did a giant belly flop into the water. Instantly he began screaming and begging to be saved. He forgot he couldn't swim.

GUILTY!

In a deep bellowing voice, a judge called the next case: People versus Samuel Perry Crook. The bailiff opened the door to the holding cell and yelled, 'Crook, come forward!' Five keen prisoners obeyed the command, jumped up, and headed for the courtroom.

NAUGHTY, NAUGHTY!

When asked for her occupation, a woman charged with a traffic violation said she was a schoolteacher. The judge rose from the bench and said, 'Madam, I have waited years for a schoolteacher to appear before this court', and smiled with delight. 'Now sit down at that table and write "I will not go through a red light" 500 times.'

YOU'LL NEVER CATCH ME!

An eccentric in a small town was well known to police for a long list of misdemeanors. He was deft at avoiding being captured. Whenever he did something stupid, he would race home to his junkyard, lock the gates, and refuse to come out. In order to avoid an unnecessary siege, the police mostly backed down and just let him stay inside. One day, however, a worker at the courthouse noticed that this guy's name came up on the list to be sent a summons for jury duty. She joked about it with officials, saying that there wasn't a hope he would come out of his junkyard fortress and she should probably just throw the summons away. But the deputy told her to send it anyway. On the day the jury convened, who should show up but our hideaway hero, who was promptly arrested and hauled off to jail.

BIG TIME CRIME

A major underworld crime figure finally met his match. He may never get out of jail after the district attorney recommended that his bail be set at 'a zillion dollars'. The judge agreed.

WITH FRIENDS LIKE THAT ...

A man charged with car theft was told by the magistrate that he could be 'tried by his peers' or appear before the magistrate alone. The man didn't know what 'peers' meant, so the magistrate explained that they were people like him. 'Try the case on your own,' said the man. 'I don't want to be tried by a bunch of car thieves.'

FINAL APPEARANCE

A lawyer was representing a client on trial for murder. His argument was that the victim—not the accused—had shot himself accidentally. To prove this, he demonstrated the victim's assumed method of drawing his gun and firing. Sorry, bud, but the gun was loaded.

IF I HAD BEEN THERE ...

A hot-headed 42-year-old man on trial for armed robbery of a store was not satisfied with his lawyer's services, so he sacked him and announced that he would represent himself. It was a difficult role but he wasn't doing a bad job, until his temper got the better of him. When the store manager stood up, looked straight at the accused, and testified that he was indeed the robber, the man jumped to his feet in a rage and roared, 'I should have blown your fucking head off ... [embarrassed pause] if I had been there.' It took 20 minutes, but the jury found him guilty.

GOODBYE $12 MILLION!

A known drug trafficker—let's call him The Big G—won $12 million in a lottery ... but had to give it all back! A week after his win, the Big G was sprung by an informant. He was recorded delivering 36 grams of cocaine and discussing his 20-year involvement in drug trafficking. He also (unwisely) told the informant that he had more cocaine at his apartment. So, police raided his place the next day and found an additional 1.63 kilograms of cocaine hidden in the dishwasher and pantry. Is this the kind of man who should be entitled to his winnings? Yes, argued his lawyer humbly, 'We're disappointed that the jury could not separate the difference between lottery proceeds, which are legitimate, and the Big G's illegal activities.' The Big G's legal team tried hard to prove that the Big G had bought the lottery ticket with money he had earned selling used clothing, but the jury was not entirely convinced. In a final attempt to let them all know what a swell guy the Big G was, his lawyer told them, with the straightest face he could muster, that with his winnings, the Big G planned to help those less fortunate than himself. He intended to use his winnings to build low-income housing ... and not to buy drugs! The jury was not impressed by his great humanitarian gesture, especially since the Big G had not filed or paid any income tax since 1989. It's not cheery what he faces: possible life imprisonment and a $4 million fine.

GO DUTCH!

If you want to succumb to a life of crime, move to the Netherlands! In a landmark case, a Dutch court ruled that a bank robber be allowed to claim the cost of a pistol used in a hold-up as a legitimate business expense. Naturally, the court insisted on receipts, invoices, or other forms of proof when calculating how much to confiscate from the convicted criminal.

When an official was asked whether a drug dealer could claim his Ferrari, he replied that he would have to prove that he needed the car to transport the drugs around. This whole concept may seem a tad liberal to some, but the Dutch court is adamant that two strict conditions must be met: one, a criminal's costs must be directly related to the crime, and not just day-to-day expenses; and two, a criminal offence must be carried out. Crime doesn't pay, but at least you can claim your expenses.

PROTESTANT WORK ETHIC?

A man was standing trial for breaking into parking meters and stealing the coins. His defence was that he was out of work and didn't go on the dole because he didn't think it was right. As he so aptly put it, 'I don't believe you have a right to money without working for it.'

INNOCENT UNTIL PROVEN GUILTY?

A man was acquitted of car theft. He told the judge that he knew he was innocent because he had been in prison at the time. When asked why on earth he hadn't brought that up at the trial, he said that he didn't want to prejudice his case.

RAISE YOUR HANDS!

Two suspects—untrained in the ways of the legal profession—were sitting at the defendant's table in a courtroom. They were nervous; it was their first time in court and the first witness was on the stand.

'Now ma'am,' began the prosecutor, 'you say you were robbed of your purse on the street?'

'Yes sir,' the witness answered.

The prosecutor continued, 'And the two men who robbed you, are they here in the courtroom today?'

Before the witness could answer, both defendants raised their hands and the judge and jury burst out laughing. Let's just do a retake, boys!

BAD IDEA

A crim broke out of jail and then a few days later went to court with his girlfriend where she was on trial for robbery. Bad idea. During the lunchbreak, he went out for a sandwich but she needed to see him, so she had him paged. Several sets of police ears pricked up as they recognised his name being broadcast over the loud speaker. They arrested him as he returned to the courthouse with his sandwich ... in a car he had stolen during the lunchbreak!

FOOT IN MOUTH DISEASE?

A man with a long history of petty thefts was up on a minor charge of allegedly stealing a VCR. When it was his chance to plead, he stood up and said, 'Not guilty, your Honour. Honestly, I didn't steal the VCR. He gave it to me because he owed me for crack.' Much to his surprise, the fellow is now serving a much longer sentence.

HEY FELLA, YOU NEED LEGAL ADVICE!

An accused bank robber decided to stand trial, acting as his own defence lawyer. No one in court that day could explain why he inexplicably called his brother as a character witness. You see, in a previous trial, his brother had pleaded guilty to being his partner-in-crime on four different occasions. What did this dimwit ask his brother? Whether he had ever committed any crimes. His brother responded, 'Yeah. You were with me on four different bank robberies. You know that.' Well, he did want the truth!

AN OLD JOKE WITH A TWIST

A lawyer defending a man accused of burglary tried this creative defense: 'My client merely inserted his arm into the window and removed a few trifling articles. His arm is not himself, and I fail to see how you can punish the whole individual for an offense committed by his limb.' 'Well put,' the judge replied. 'Using your logic, I sentence the defendant's arm to one year's imprisonment. He can accompany it or not, as he chooses.' The defendant smiled. With his lawyer's assistance he detached his artificial limb, laid it on the bench, and walked out a free man.

DON'T MESS WITH ME

Feisty folks who fight back!

What's the typical profile of a small-time crook? A little bit slow, possibly a loner, didn't get much out of school? Perhaps they have an optimistic outlook on life? They dream about wealth and success and an end to the daily grind and believe they can get out of it and rise above it. 'I'll show you I'm not a loser', they think. It's an inherently positive attitude; it's that fighting spirit that gets them going. How else could they expect to get away with the brainless things they try and do? The trouble starts when the victims of their crimes share that same fighting spirit. That's when some of these dumb crims just don't know what to do. Cheers to all those feisty folk who decide to fight back!

THERE'S A TIME AND A PLACE FOR EVERYTHING

A man and a woman got into a brawl at a bar over a mobile phone. The woman snatched it away from the man, and he tried to grab it back. A police officer came over to separate them and hear both sides of the story. The young woman was only too happy to be as vindictive as she could be. She told the police officer that she had loaned her friend $125 for his phone bill and all she wanted was her money back; she was sick and tired of asking him over and over again. Then, to rub it in, she told the officer that her friend had been involved in a robbery. The man jumped in, quick to deny it, and tried to make out that she was a little bit round the twist. Bad move. This comment made her really flip and she became even more determined to get her revenge. So, she told the officer that the man had shown her a picture on his mobile phone of him with a gun ... and wouldn't you know it, there he was proud as punch with a nice shiny gun. The man was cornered; the photographic evidence was on the table. He confessed that he had been the getaway driver in a recent bank heist. He also wished that they hadn't gone out for a drink that night.

ZUT ALORS!

A professional French pickpocket used astoundingly poor judgment when selecting his most recent victim at the Seville Airport. The thief, who specialises in international events that attract crowds of visitors, thought he was in his element when he circled a group of young men and chose his prey. Little did he realise that he was dipping into the bag of Larry Wade, champion 110-metre hurdler for the US Athletics team. He was spotted by Maurice Green, the fastest sprinter in the world, capable of running 100 metres in 9.79 seconds. Despite his considerable head start, the two athletes quickly chased him down. The pickpocket pretended that he was just an innocent French tourist who knew nothing, but the entire episode was captured on film by a Spanish television crew that had been interviewing Mr Green at the time.

WHEN YOU GOTTA GO, YOU GOTTA GO

One Sunday morning, a 30-year-old man forced his way into the home of an 87-year-old man. Threatening the old man with a gun, the 30-year-old asked for cash. The elderly victim found a small amount of money and then asked if he could go to the toilet. The robber agreed. Quick smart, or at least as fast as he could, the sprightly old fellow climbed out the window and called police from the neighbour's house.

FLYING APPLE STRUDELS

For those with a liking for coffee and croissants, a patisserie is an ideal target. At least, theoretically, as a couple of would-be crooks discovered. When they made a brave attempt to rob one such store, the 65-year-old owner, her daughter, and two grandchildren pelted the crooks with pastries and chased them away.

HOME SWEET HOME

In the dead of night, a would-be thief broke into a couple's home and demanded cash. Realising he was a few sandwiches short of a picnic, they told him they didn't have much money and they'd have to wait until the bank opened in the morning so they could make a withdrawal. The crook agreed and was quite taken by the hospitality of the homeowners. They gave him dinner, let him have a shower and watch TV ... and then fall fast asleep. Police arrived to find him snoring peacefully on the couch.

PEEK-A-BOO—WE SEE YOU!

Two relatively inexperienced robbers decided to rob their local pizza joint. They rocked up to the front of the shop and put their masks on—in full view of the manager, who watched the whole thing through the plate glass window. Primed and ready for them when they burst in, the manager managed to belt one of them in the head and a mighty punch-up ensued. A little later, robber no.1 was seen rushing robber no.2 to hospital where they were taken into custody.

NIGHTY NIGHT!

A would-be hostage-taker learned two important rules of criminal conduct the hard way: don't go into a house where you're outnumbered, and don't fall asleep on the job. The 18-year-old committed a string of robberies and then to top it off, broke into an apartment where he held three hostages at gunpoint. But after two hours of heavy drinking, he passed out on the couch. The hostages took his gun away, called police, and breathed a sigh of relief.

DON'T MESS WITH GRANNY

An elderly woman spent a leisurely morning shopping in one of those shopping centres where there are so many parking levels that it takes you half an hour to find your car. Returning to her vehicle, she found four strange men inside—two in the front and two in the back. She was terrified but reacted quickly. Holding up one of her plastic bags, she pretended she had a gun inside—it was actually a banana! She pointed it at the men and calmly told them that if they did not get out of the car, she would shoot. The four men skedaddled. Shaking, the lady got into the car and sat quietly, giving herself a chance to calm down. After a couple of minutes, she felt okay to drive. She tried to start the car but her key didn't fit. She thought it was just nerves. She tried again. The key still didn't fit. Then to her horror, she realised it wasn't her car at all—her identical car was parked three spaces further along. Terribly embarrassed, she drove to the nearest police station and explained her story. The officer on duty laughed heartily and pointed to the other end of the counter. Who did she see? Four pale, wide-eyed men reporting a hijacking by a mean old lady!

DON'T TRY THIS AT HOME, KIDS!

Late one night, a young girl saw a car pull up slowly in front of her driveway. Three men jumped out and ran towards the garage. She called her mum and older sister, but mum wasn't phased. She just said to flick on the lights a few times to scare them away, but her diminutive five-foot, 17-year-old sister decided to take a closer look. She went downstairs, heard noises, opened the garage door, and saw someone running away. Then she took off after him. The tiny teen ran about 100 metres before catching one of the men and tackling him on the grass. She then yelled for her mum to bring a dog leash, which she used to wrap up the failed cat burglar until police arrived. Don't try this at home kids, unless you have a lot of athletics training up your belt to help you outrun a crook.

STICKY END

A would-be thief broke into a house armed with duct tape. He was going to tie up the inhabitants and rob them. But two next-door neighbours heard the teenage daughter scream as he burst into the house. They went to investigate and found the girl and her grandmother struggling. Two against one was too much for him—they overpowered the unsuccessful thief and used his duct tape to attach him securely to the washing line until police arrived.

BRAINLESS CROOK GETS BRAINED!

A robber wielding a knife burst into a jewellery store and demanded $5000. The owner calmly replied that he didn't have the money on hand and began to negotiate with the thief. While this was going on, the owner's wife crept up behind him with a rolling pin. At the last moment he spun round only to be clubbed on the head by the owner who had managed to grab a brass-handled walking stick. Husband and wife then attacked the thief with such gusto that the walking stick snapped. The terrified thief struggled to his feet and fled with nothing.

SINGIN' IN THE RAIN?

A man who grabbed an elderly lady's handbag got more than he bargained for when she whacked him over the head with her umbrella. A witness chased the man, who was last seen disappearing into casualty at the nearby hospital.

LOOK BEHIND YOU

A man walked into a bank, pulled out a pistol, and demanded money. He started to fill his jacket pockets with his left hand while holding the gun in his right. The man directly behind him looked over his shoulder and saw that the hammer was down. He drew a .38 revolver and placed it in his back saying, 'You cock that gun and you're a dead man.' It turned out that the man behind him was an FBI agent waiting to cash his pay cheque.

SAMURAI SURPRISE!

A man was spotted driving a stolen car at 7.15 p.m. one night when police attempted to pull him over. He led officers on a high-speed chase before crashing into two cars at an intersection. He leapt from the car and ran down a residential street into someone's front yard. From there he dashed round the back and found the back door open. Salvation? No. The car thief didn't count on being accosted by the homeowner who happened to have a display of oriental weapons on his wall. The owner grabbed a Samurai sword and swished and swirled and terrorised the thief until police arrived to take over in a more sedate manner.

GREY POWER!

A 72-year-old man who had spent 23 years of his life in jail thought he was in the clear. He walked into a bank, ran out moments later with a stack of stolen cash, and headed back to his mini-van to get away. However, a feisty lady, who also happened to be 72 years old, was sitting in a car waiting for her daughter-in-law to come out from the post office when she saw the man run from the bank with several employees in pursuit. So leaving her daughter-in-law far behind, she stepped on the accelerator and chased the elderly gent in her car for over 10 kilometres and called police with his whereabouts. Minutes later police arrived to find her giving the thief a piece of her mind. 'He's a silly old coot', she told police and they agreed.

CAPELESS CRUSADER!

An inexperienced teenage cat burglar got more than he bargained for when he broke into a stranger's home. The man was asleep when he heard noises around midnight. He leapt up and confronted the cat burglar by grabbing him, stripping him to his underpants, and tying him up with duct tape. Police diplomatically said he went a bit too far in his personal crusade against crime, but he had a good reason why he didn't want police to come sniffing around—he didn't want them to find the hydroponic marijuana operation he had going!

MOTHER ANGEL DARLING?

The ties between mother and daughter are incredibly strong, but it seems they can be broken ... if the price is right. When a 19-year-old lady was arrested on a domestic violence-related charge, her mother went to the jail and posted a $5000 bond. She then had a change of heart and wanted her money back. The mother hired a thug to go round to her daughter's place to bring her to her home.

The hired hand went round to the daughter's house, banged on the door, and yelled for someone open up. He falsely claimed he had a warrant for her arrest and told the residents that their home was surrounded. It wasn't—there was just him—but it sounded good. The thug stormed in, handcuffed the daughter, and then drove her to a meeting with her mother where he turned her over with the handcuffs still on. The mother then drove her daughter to the jail to get her bond money back. Didn't she get a surprise! Instead of giving the mother her money back, authorities called investigators. Mum and the thug were arrested for criminal trespassing, unauthorised entry of an inhabited dwelling, false imprisonment, and false impersonation. No one knows just what the daughter thoughtof all this.

ALOHA, LITTLE BRAT!

A 13-year-old teenage boy went on a real 'joy-flight' to Hawaii and back all in one day! He charged the airline ticket online to his mother's credit card and got himself to the airport and on board the flight to Maui. He was booked on a return flight that arrived in time for him to be home before midnight, so he figured (naively!) that his mum wouldn't notice. But she did! Realising he was missing, she checked their home computer and found that he had ordered the plane ticket. Wasn't he surprised when police were waiting at the arrivals gate to escort him home. No charges, but his mother sentenced him to two years' hard labour!

HEY GUYS, IT'S ONLY PAINT!

For a prank, two naive teenagers hopped in a car and drove round the neighborhood armed with paintball guns, helmets and paintball vests. They first pelted some children at a playground then they shot at another group of youths down the street. When the teens slowed down to tell them they were only shooting paintballs, one of the group on the footpath pulled out a gun and returned fire with more than a dozen bullets. The teens drove themselves to hospital—one was shot in the left arm, and the other in the buttocks. They learnt a valuable lesson: some people just don't see the funny side of things, do they?

GOOD OLD HAM SANDWICHES

A man burst through a kitchen window with a sawed-off shotgun one night. The owners—two women in their sixties—were taken aback but decided to take a soft approach and try to befriend him. So they showered him with kindness, first suggesting a bath and a shave, and then plying him with ham sandwiches, gin and tonic, and scotch on the rocks. He never said what he wanted, but just sat with them, holding his gun, until he finally passed out on the sofa. Police arrived soon after to end the bizarre five-hour episode.

BULLETPROOF BELLY LAUGH

Sometimes bank robbers can be scared off by the darnedest things. When a masked man pulled out a gun at a young bank teller, she just laughed in his face. The suspect was so humiliated that he spun round and ran away. The teller had no fear for one simple reason— she knew she was protected by bulletproof glass.

YOU GUYS CRACK ME UP!

A motorist was caught in a fixed camera radar speed trap. He didn't realise he was in the wrong until he received an official letter in the mail with a photo of his car sent as proof and a fine for $67. Being a bit of a smart arse, instead of just sending a cheque back to the police department to pay for the fine, he sent them a photograph of $67. Several days later, he received another letter from the police department that contained another picture ... of handcuffs. He paid up.

WHERE THERE'S SMOKE ...

A rather cunning middle-aged man, having purchased a case of very rare, very expensive cigars, insured them against fire, among other things. Within a month, having smoked his entire stockpile of cigars and without having made even his first premium payment on the policy, the man filed a claim against the insurance company. In his claim, the man stated the cigars were lost 'in a series of small fires'. The insurance company refused to pay, citing the obvious reason—the man had simply smoked them! The man sued and—would you believe it—won the case. In delivering the ruling the judge agreed that the claim was frivolous but, nevertheless, the man did hold a policy from the company in which it had warranted that the cigars were insurable and also guaranteed that it would insure against fire, without defining what it considered to be 'unacceptable fire'. On this basis, they were obligated to pay the claim.

Rather than endure a lengthy and costly appeal process, the insurance company accepted the ruling and paid the man $15 000 for the rare cigars he lost 'in a series of small fires'. After the man cashed the cheque, however, the tables were turned. You see the company had the man arrested on 24 counts of arson. With his own insurance claim and testimony from the previous case being used against him, the man was convicted of intentionally burning his insured property. His reward? Twenty-four months in jail and a $24 000 fine. Interestingly, that's one month in jail and $1000 dollars for each of those cigars!

QUIT WHILE YOU'RE AHEAD

Kidnappers abducted a wealthy factory owner from outside his factory late one afternoon and then demanded $690 000 in ransom money. But during the night, the victim managed to escape and return home. The next morning, he got a phone call from the kidnappers. They wanted $11 500 to defray the cost of the abduction. The factory owner played along with them and even managed to negotiate a 50 per cent reduction in the cost! They agreed on a time and a place to meet to hand over the money. The knuckleheads didn't think for one moment that the police might show up too.

CHARMING

Prostitution is still illegal, although some people don't seem to think so. A man rang police to complain that the service he had received from an escort agency was not satisfactory—in fact, the prostitute and her pimp had ripped him off. He had booked the services of a prostitute through the escort agency's brochure but when she came to the door he took one look at her and told her to forget it. Apparently her pimp wasn't very happy about that so he broke down the door and took his money. The man was very indignant. As he said as he was reporting this humiliating crime: 'I'm not going to pay for that! She's dog ugly.'

POW POW PEPPERONI!

A man tried to rob a deli, but he didn't get far—the owner broke his nose by hitting him with a giant salami!

REALLY BAD DRIVERS

Wham bam thank you ma'am!

Speeding is one of the most common ways to be caught on the road. But there are plenty of people out there who come up with much more original offences to be charged with! They deliberately ram their ex-lover's car, they plough through department store windows or, in an alcoholic haze, end up driving onto a runway where there's a jet ready to take off. Really bad drivers have the knack of making a spectacle of themselves ... and make you wanna scream and shout, especially when they run into you.

GIVE ME MY SPEEDING TICKET!

A young police officer clocked a motorist in an old Studebaker Lark doing 87 kilometres per hour in a 60 zone. The elderly gentleman at the wheel was very polite and readily admitted he was speeding. To reward him for his honesty, the police officer told him he would write him a ticket for driving 75 kilometres in a 60 zone, which meant he would avoid a court appearance. The man strenuously objected to the reduced speeding ticket. 'The guys I work with keep telling me my Studebaker can't go over 80,' he explained, 'so I wanna prove them wrong!' The officer obliged, writing him a ticket for the more serious traffic offence. The man was as happy as Larry.

BATTLE OF THE LIMOS

A radio call went out at 7.45 a.m. one morning asking police officers to look out for two white limousines smashing into each other during a violent chase. A witness directed police to the scene where one of the late-model limos sat with a crumpled rear end, its driver—a male—lying on the ground in tears. The man said that he and his wife of three years had separated but were trying to reconcile. She was visiting him but they had several arguments so he told her he'd had enough and left. He was having a beer and watching TV in the back seat of his limousine with a female friend when his wife arrived. She drove up in another limo the couple owned together, became enraged and slammed her limo into her husband's one several times before her husband tried to escape. When he drove off, his wife followed, ramming him five to seven times during a pursuit that reached speeds of 110 kilometres per hour. The wife was handcuffed at the scene next to the car she was driving, which was missing the front grill and had a damaged headlight. She pleaded not guilty to multiple charges, including assault with a dangerous weapon and driving to endanger. As for mending his relationship with his wife, all the shaken man could say was, 'She's a scary lady.'

PEUGEOT PUNCH-UP

Police responded to a motor vehicle accident and found both occupants unconscious in the back seat. It seems the driver of the car, who was intoxicated, objected to something his passenger had said, so he punched him in the face. The passenger then scrambled into the back seat to get away. Did the driver stop the car and deal with it? No. He followed him over the front seat to the back while the car was still moving. The now driver-less car continued merrily on its way before crashing into some trees. The bickering buddies were taken to hospital with minor injuries.

HONEST BUT STUPID!

An officer stopped a vehicle for speeding and weaving from one side of the road to the other. Clearly the driver was intoxicated. After collecting the offender's driver's licence, the officer returned to his patrol car. He was on the radio with his station when he heard an engine start and, looking up, saw the vehicle tearing off at a high speed. After a short chase, the police officer once again had the man in custody. He asked the driver why he had taken off. 'For the thrill of it!' the man beamed before getting slapped with further charges.

LET'S PLAY HORSIES!

A police patrol car pulled over a vehicle that was changing lanes erratically. Expecting to find an inebriated driver inside, the officers were surprised to discover two of them—one in the driver's seat and one on the driver's lap—facing the wrong way. No, they weren't indulging in a passionate encounter. Seems they were attempting to swap places while driving in the mistaken belief that the passenger was less drunk than the driver. He wasn't.

WORLD CHAMPION CAR DRIVER

A not-too-bright youth finally got his driver's licence after four attempts. Proudly driving home from the motor registry in his dad's car, he lost concentration as he was changing a cassette and ended up ploughing through the front fence of someone's house. Leaping out and having a good look around, he didn't see anyone so he simply drove home, being a bit more careful. He was very surprised when a police officer arrived at his door about an hour later with his bumper bar and car numberplate tucked neatly under his arm. He had held his driver's licence for the impressively short time of four hours ... anyone beat that?

THE NIGHT I WISHED I STAYED AT HOME

One night when his parents were out, a teenage boy invited some mates around and got stuck into some heavy under-age drinking. When they ran out of alcohol, the boy decided to take the family car down to the local liquor store to buy some more. He wasn't old enough to have a driver's licence, but with his alcohol-induced bravado, he didn't care. Of course, he didn't have any proof of age either, so the liquor store owner refused to sell him anything. He left irritated and empty-handed, only to find that the car wouldn't start. Starting to get that sinking feeling that he was going to be in serious trouble if he did not get home, he decided to steal a police car that was parked nearby! As he was driving home, who should cruise by on the other side of the road but another police patrol car. After doing a double-take at the person in the driver's seat, the police car started its sirens, did a U-turn and went in pursuit. Did the boy take off in a madcap chase? Nah. He was thoroughly defeated by this stage, so he let them take him home in their car. And then he let his mum and dad take him to the police station. And then he went to court.

KEEP YOUR EYES ON THE ROAD

Police responded to a call about a car that was reportedly weaving in and out of its lane and changing speed erratically. Police discovered that the driver was not concentrating too hard on driving, but that while he was at the wheel, he was simultaneously watching a porno movie on a portable DVD player. Unfortunately for him, the DVD player (and a lot of other goods in the car) turned out to be stolen. He was taken into custody and never did get to see the end of the movie.

WRONG WAY, LADY

A woman was charged with drink driving and trespassing after she drove onto a runway at an international airport. A Boeing 737, in the process of taking off, had to move to the side of the runway to avoid hitting her car. Later, down at the friendly police station, she claimed that she had no idea where she was, but she did begin to wonder why there were so few people around.

SUPERSONIC STUPIDITY!

A highway patrol in Arizona was mystified when it came across a pile of smouldering wreckage embedded in the side of a cliff rising above a road. Bits of metal and other debris suggested that this was the site of a plane crash, but lab results revealed something quite odd ... it was the vaporised remains of a car. How does a car driving along a road suddenly vaporise? Well, the pieces fitted together something like this.

It seems that an ex-air force sergeant stole a Jet Assisted Take-Off Unit, known as JATO. JATO units are solid fuel rockets used to give heavy military transport airplanes an extra push for take-off from short airfields. The second thing that is crucial to this tale is the fact that dried desert lakebeds are the location of choice for breaking the world ground vehicle speed record. So, armed with that information, the sergeant took the JATO unit into the Arizona desert and found a long, straight stretch of road. He attached the JATO unit to his 1967 Chevy, jumped in, accelerated to a high speed and fired off the rocket. The Chevy tore down the highway reaching speeds of 400–480 kilometres per hour for approximately 15 to 20 seconds before the sergeant applied the brakes. This did not have the desired effect. Trying to brake completely melted the brakes, blew the tyres, and left thick rubber marks on the road surface. The vehicle then became airborne for two kilometres, smashed into the cliff face, and left a two-metre crater in the rock.

NO TRESPASSING

A cyclist crossing an airport runway came to an untimely end when he was hit by a plane coming in to land. He didn't hear the twin-engine aircraft because he was groovin' along to his walkman. He would have been charged with trespassing if he'd been smart enough to survive.

NOT INTO THE WINDOW, STUPID!

A police officer walking down the street on patrol saw a car driving crazily down the main street of town at a very slow speed. The officer shouted, 'Pull over, driver!' He did, by driving the car up onto the footpath and crashing it through the plate glass windows of a large department store.

SOME PEOPLE NEVER LEARN!

A prisoner was released from jail where he had served a sentence for drink driving, auto theft, and habitually driving with a suspended or revoked licence. Four days later, he returned to the jail to pick up his belongings—and that's when his nightmare started. Asked to provide ID, he gave the official his licence, which after a routine computer check, was found to have been revoked for life. The official couldn't accuse him of doing anything illegal without seeing him behind the wheel, but she didn't have to wait long. He told her he'd be back and she watched as he got into the car, parked in a no standing zone and came back inside to claim his clothing, shampoo, dartboard and battery charger. A further computer check of the car's registration found that it had been reported stolen the same day the jailbird was released from jail. He was handcuffed and arrested just as he was about to drive away. Back in jail, he was charged with auto theft and habitually driving with a suspended or revoked licence.

DON'T FOLLOW THE LIGHTS!

A drunk driver was on his way to meet some friends at a restaurant to celebrate his birthday. The venue was a popular meeting place, well known for miles around and brightly illuminated at night. It's situated at the end of a long straight road with a sharp curve just before it crosses a river. Our fearless driver, seeing the bright lights up ahead, drove towards them and straight into the river. This didn't stop him from getting to the party though, grinning from ear to ear, and covered up to his chest in thick black mud.

TAKE THAT AND THAT AND THAT!

Police responded to reports of a collision and arrived at the scene to find a young woman who readily told them that she had rammed the car in front of her three times. She explained that it was her boyfriend's car and she was mad at him because she had gone over to his place and found him with another woman. Hmm. There was just one problem—the car in front of her did not belong to her boyfriend; it belonged to a complete stranger who was innocently on his way to work when he was slammed from behind. Turned out the young lady wasn't a whiz at observation. She got the model right but the colour, well ... her boyfriend's car was maroon and this one was bright red.

GREEN FOR GO, RED FOR STOP

This tale takes place in a small country town without any traffic lights. A police officer on duty was sitting in a marked car on the side of the main road. A car pulled off the road and stopped behind him with its headlights and engine still on. When the driver didn't get out of the car, the police officer went over to make sure everything was all right. He asked the driver why he had stopped and the driver replied, 'I'm just waiting for the light to change, officer.' He was immediately arrested for drink driving.

QUIT WHILE YOU'RE AHEAD

A man attempted to steal a trailer from an equipment hire company. He drove in, hitched a trailer onto the back of his van and drove off quickly, only to crash a couple of kilometres down the road. Not giving up easily, he went back to the hire company, hitched up a second trailer and drove off, only to have it come loose and crash 50 metres away from the first one. A police car on patrol noticed two trailers on the side of the road and stopped to investigate. Just then the hapless trailer thief drove by with his third stolen trailer, and managed to side-swipe the stationary police car. A wacky 25-kilometre chase ensued which, by then, the trailer thief was canny enough to realise that trailers fall off at high speeds!

FORGOT TO PAY, OFFICER!

At a service station one afternoon, a guy filled his car with petrol and then decided to cruise out without paying. He taunted the service station attendant and gave him the finger as he went past. The attendant ran out to get the guy's numberplate and was pleased to see the car crash straight into a police car!

WHAM BAM THANK YOU MA'AM!

A female motorist angry about getting a $90 speeding ticket slammed her red Mazda into the police officer's vehicle several times. At first, when the 20-year-old woman was pulled over for speeding, she signed the ticket without complaint. The officer got back in his car and both cars pulled away, but as he was about to make a right-hand turn, he saw the red Mazda speed up behind him and deliberately slam into the back. Police say the woman rear-ended the police car three more times, then zoomed past, turned around and hit it head-on. The officer finally pinned her car to the kerb with his car. Now the woman faces an assault charge on top of her speeding ticket. Not a smart move, ma'am, if you ask me.

NUDE DRIVING–THE LATEST CRAZE?

A semi driver who was changing his clothes while driving along a motorway rolled his truck while going around a notorious curve. No other vehicles or people were involved, but the accident resulted in police shutting down the highway for more than three hours. Climbing out of his truck after the accident, the embarrassed driver—who was completely starkers—told police he had set the cruise control to 90 kilometres per hour and was changing his clothes when he approached the curve. He misjudged the turn, causing his truck to roll off the road and damage two fences. He was taken to hospital, in the nude, but was not seriously hurt.

STEP ON IT!

Two guys decided to rob a bank which was located at an intersection. One of the crooks was waiting in the getaway car with the motor running; the other guy was inside committing the robbery. When the robber came out of the bank he jumped in the car and told his driver to hit the accelerator. He did. Problem was, he put the car in reverse, pushed his foot to the floor, and crashed into a police car that was coming up the street.

BABY, YOU CAN DRIVE MY CAR

This particular 'criminal' is too young to be charged, but his mum deserves a good kick in the bum! Police apprehended a four-year-old boy driving his mother's car to a video shop in the middle of the night. Although he was unable to reach the accelerator, the boy managed to drive to the store, 400 metres from his home, at about 1.30 a.m. one Friday. Headlights off, the car wove along the street precariously and attracted the attention of police—especially when it struck two parked cars. The boy was able to put the vehicle in reverse, but then ran it into the back of the police car. Police returned the little speedster to his mother, who told police she had previously let him steer from her lap. Perhaps her son should learn to ride a scooter first.

OFFICER, ARREST THAT MAN!

A guy pulled up to a police car and pointed out a car that had been speeding. The driver claimed the car had been doing 80 kilometres per hour in a 60 zone. The police officer duly issued a ticket to the man himself. You see, he admitted to clocking the car; he could only do that if he was speeding himself. And secondly, the police officer wasn't going to book the car in question—it was an unmarked police car responding to a call.

ZERO TO 60 IN 10 MINUTES FLAT!

A man was driving his Ford Escort a little too fast. It's a reliable car, but not especially strong in the acceleration department. Seeing that he was about to be pulled over, the man decided to try and outrun the police. He forgot two important things: one, a police sedan will invariably accelerate more rapidly than your average Ford Escort; and two, every road leading out of this particular town happened to be uphill. Needless to say, the man was caught easily and charged—not only with speeding, but with reckless driving and resisting arrest.

LET ME OUT OF HERE!

Things that go terribly wrong!

It's no surprise that a lot of criminals don't plan ahead. They have what they think is a great idea—usually fuelled by drugs or alcohol—and they go for it. And often they get what they want—at least to start with—but then it's the aftermath of the crime when it all begins to unravel. Some crims forget to organise a getaway car, or forget to fill the petrol tank of their getaway car, or hire a driver who can't drive! And then, when they realise it's really happening, the police are after them and they have to run and hide. Where do they go? Here are some tortured tales about not-too-bright thieves who find themselves stuck in awkward situations—stuck like a fly on a piece of flypaper when things go terribly wrong.

VIEW'S NICE FROM UP HERE

A plumpish jail inmate was sick and tired of being in jail, so without much thought, he made a break for it by climbing out his window. He got stuck, as these things sometimes happen, and couldn't get himself loose. The guards couldn't get him loose either, so it was up to the fire brigade to come to the rescue. Our slightly squished inmate has now been moved to a cell without a window.

IF THERE'S A WAY IN, THERE'S A WAY OUT

A would-be robber came down an air vent and landed right in the middle of a large electrical goods store. Immediately the motion sensor siren went off—it was deafeningly loud and the robber at that point just wanted to get the hell out of there. He tried to stack some cardboard boxes up to climb out the air vent but they weren't sturdy enough. Going mad from the noise, he suddenly realised that the cops had arrived. Quickly he lay down on the floor right next to the wall, evidently hoping they wouldn't see him. Too bad they did see him, but even more, too bad he didn't know that he could have just lifted up the security bar and vanished out the back door.

IT'S DARK IN HERE

A robber fled from a bank and jumped into the boot of a parked car, thinking that no-one would find him. He was right ... he wasn't found for almost a week. After five days, cramped, dirty and scared, his whimpering and hollering brought relief. The owner of the car heard his cries and opened the boot. The trouble is that the car belonged to an undercover police team that was trailing another criminal.

WHY DON'T I TURN MYSELF IN?

A man decided to rob a local bar. He figured, as a lot of dumb crooks do, that the best way to avoid being seen, was to climb onto the roof and slide in through an air vent. Once inside the airconditioning system, he realised it would be too difficult to try to get back out the same way, so he tried to break the windows. Unfortunately for him, it was shatterproof glass. With no way out and not keen to spend the night stuck in an air vent, our fearless burglar rang the police and got them to rescue him.

OOOOPS, WRONG CAR!

Three armed bandits surrounded a car and demanded money. They didn't realise that in the car was the president's son. The car behind was full of presidential bodyguards and the three surrounded bandits weren't exactly happy to see them.

SMOKE GETS IN YOUR EYES

A man breaks into an old farmhouse to see if there's anything worth stealing. Since it's pretty deserted and it's cold outside, the man decides to sleep there for the night. It's an old house with not much in the way of a heating system, so he decides to light a fire. What he doesn't know is that the chimneys are covered to prevent possums from getting in. The man makes his fire, goes to sleep, and wakes up to find the house burning down around him. He just escapes by the hair on his chinny chin chin!

THE OTHER SIDE OF THE FENCE

After robbing a convenience store, two teenage boys were chased by a security guard. Desperately trying to escape, they scrambled over a three-metre chain-link fence. They beamed when they looked back to see the guard standing there, not even trying to follow them. You see he didn't have to—they had just climbed over the fence into a mini-mum-security jail.

NOT A GOOD HIDING PLACE

Laundry workers in an upmarket hotel were puzzled when they noticed that no laundry was reaching the bottom of the 20-storey laundry chute. The answer soon became apparent when one of them saw two feet poking through an opening in the chute—they belonged to a man wanted for questioning over a series of jewellery store robberies.

IT'S DARK IN HERE

One morning the cleaner in a pharmacy heard strange strangled noises coming from above him. After looking in various places, he realised that the noise was coming from the airconditioning system. A thief had entered the ventilation system in the middle of the night but got stuck. Four hours later, police were happy to un-stick him.

PONG!

Three robbers escaped from a bank, jumped into the getaway car, and roared off. Police were able to follow them to a quiet suburban street, where they began a door knock. After their efforts were proving fruitless they decided to search one last house. From over their heads, a shout of absolute horror rang out, 'Aaaah!' Turned out, the three robbers were safely ensconced in the attic ... until they found a dead body. The tenant of the house explained later that she had complained to the landlord about a funny smell.

CAREFUL WHERE YOU STUFF THAT MONEY!

A man casually dressed in T-shirt and shorts walked into a bank and jogged out two minutes later with a bag full of cash. He set off down the street, jogging at an easy pace, with the moneybag stuffed down the front of his shorts. He was feeling pretty pleased—he fitted into the scene perfectly. To any police around, he looked just like any other jogger out and about on a beautiful spring morning. That is until the moneybag exploded, covering his nether regions with bright red dye.

GRRRR ... NICE DOGGIE!

After a spree of kidnapping, armed robbery, auto theft, and other offences, a 17-year-old led police on a high-speed chase down the freeway. He exited the freeway but found himself caught in a dead-end street. He tried to ram his vehicle through a high wire fence but couldn't do it, so he jumped out of the car and scaled the fence himself ... only to find he had landed inside a police dog compound. Dogs one, youth zero.

CHUTE!

A cat burglar abseiled down the side of an apartment building to enter an open window but was spotted by a security guard. He successfully evaded searchers by hiding in the building's ninth-floor rubbish chute. However, when he attempted to escape by using the chute to get down to the basement, he got stuck on the sixth floor where the chute narrowed to less than half a square metre. It took a rescue team with jackhammers and metal shears four hours to open a hole in the reinforced concrete to get him out.

HIDE AND SEEK

Police called in dogs to track a suspect wanted in connection with a high-speed chase along winding country roads. The chase ended when the suspect crashed the car and fled on foot into a nearby field. Police, tracker dogs, and the farmer who owned the property went on an intensive search. The suspect was probably relieved to be caught—he spent one and a half hours hiding in a pile of manure.

I DON'T FEEL SAFE!

Two men broke into a hotel by smashing a ground floor window. Once inside they found two empty cash registers ... and a safe. Safes are pretty heavy—this one was roughly 320 kilograms—and the pair only managed to shift it about a metre along the floor before they were intercepted by police. Police, alerted by reports of smashing glass, waited outside, listening to the sounds of the two hapless men struggling with the safe. They kicked open a side door and confronted the pair. One crim was found with a large bolt cutter in his hand and a pry tool in his pocket; the second had a large knife ... explain that one, guys!

WRONG CAR, BROTHER!

A man brandishing a knife held-up a mechanics workshop and ran off down the road with an employee in pursuit. The suspect ran into a car park and, seeing his victim gaining on him, jumped into the passenger side of a cruising white car ... which happened to be an unmarked police car!

STUCK!

A couple rang police when they heard strange muffled cries coming from the church next door. It seems that someone had tried to break in. The evidence was fairly convincing—the rear end of a two-metre 145-kilogram man sticking out of a side church window. It took four police to free him—two inside pushing and two outside pulling. But it only took one to charge him with break and entering.

ARE YOU SERIOUS?

An accident-prone thief stole a bag full of cash from a bank, but it was hardly a clean getaway. After grabbing the loot from the teller, he put his handgun back in his pants pocket and it went off, startling everyone, including himself. Then he made a beeline for the front door and ran straight out onto the path of an oncoming van. The driver, unaware the man had just robbed the bank, jumped out to assist him. The feisty bandit staggered to his feet and, declining assistance from the van driver, limped over to a waiting getaway car. Phew, made it!

HEY BOSS! WHAT
ARE YOU DOING HERE?

A restaurant employee got off his shift at midnight and returned two hours later to rob the premises. He broke a window only to find the owner and another employee still inside. He picked up a meat cleaver and demanded the owner's wallet. The owner handed it over but it had no cash inside. The man then threw the meat cleaver at his boss, missing him. Now that the man was unarmed, both victims turned on him and attacked him by bashing him over the head with a chair. The would-be robber spent the next two days in hospital and the next few months in a cell.

WHO LET THE DOGS OUT?

A thief stole a car and was driving along when the owner's daughter noticed him in it. She tried to wave him down, but he swerved and drove into a ditch. He then leapt out and fled into the woods ... where there happened to be police dog training exercises going on. When he heard the ominous sounds of dogs coming towards him, the thief surrendered quick smart, saying he'd seen too many movies to mess around with police dogs.

NICE YOU COULD DROP IN!

Early one morning, police hit a house where they believed a suspect was hiding. They knocked on the door and a woman refused to open it, clearly trying to stall them from going inside by chatting to them through the bedroom window. Just then, there was a loud crash and an explosion of dust. Through the window, police saw the suspect picking himself up off the floor and making a run for it. They then entered and found a huge chunk of ceiling lying on the bedroom floor ... plus an out-of-breath suspect hiding in the kitchen.

DRIVER, PAY YOUR TOLL!

Three intoxicated young men got more than they bargained for when they sped right into a major drama. They thought they were running a tollbooth, but they were actually entering a restricted air force base. As they attempted to drive through they were surrounded by uniformed guards, machine guns and military vehicles in a matter of moments. As if that wasn't embarrassing enough, they just happened to be carrying cocaine, drug paraphernalia, and more than $1000 in cash—all laid out in full view on the front seat. It's hard to see how anyone would mistake a high-profile military outpost for an expressway tollbooth, but there you go ...

YOU NEED A GETAWAY CAR

A shoplifter ran out of a shopping centre around 7.45 p.m. one Thursday night after a police officer saw her dumping a bag filled with $286 worth of clothing into a garbage can. She scurried across a main road and into a wooded area near a quiet street. She then jumped out and attempted to flag down a car. Safe at last! Er, no ... she found herself sitting in an unmarked police car.

TAKE A PACKED LUNCH

Shortly before noon, hotel staff in a luxury hotel heard banging sounds coming from the walls and ceiling of the grand ballroom. When a staff member went to investigate, he saw a foot sticking out of an aircon-ditioning shaft. It took fire fighters 30 minutes to extricate the tall, thin and shivering man from the ducting system. He was taken to hospital suffering from dehydration. Gratitude for his rescue, however, was short-lived—he had handcuffs slapped on him immediately and was arrested on suspicion of commercial burglary. Hotel officials said they suspect that he may have been there as long as two days. Police are still waiting to hear exactly what he was doing there, because he was too shocked, cold and tired to explain.

HELLO SANTA CLAUS!

When you're found naked wedged in a chimney in the middle of the night, the excuse that you were retrieving the keys you accidentally dropped down the chimney doesn't exactly sound very convincing. But that's what one 34-year-old man told police after he was finally rescued from his hellhole.

The story began when he climbed up the single-storey building and took off his clothes to squeeze down the chimney. He then proceeded to slide down the chimney inch by inch. Now our sneaky slider was no Santa Claus, he was a very skinny guy but even so, he found himself totally stuck. A passerby heard screams for help coming from inside the store. Police were called and then the fire brigade. Firefighters broke into the chimney with sledgehammers and freed the man, who they say was lucky to be alive. If he'd been stuck in the chimney all weekend, they don't reckon he would have made it.

COSMIC KARMA?

What goes around comes around—isn't that what they say? Police responded to two car crashes within minutes of each other on the same stretch of road, which ended up having a spooky connection! The first was a hit and run; the second was when a vehicle slammed into a train. City police and firefighters responded to the second scene, where the suspect was found trapped inside his car but alive. The passenger side of the car was caved in, and both the front and rear doors were destroyed by the collision and the work performed by the rescue crew to get him out. Just as firefighters had resorted to using power tools to extricate the driver from his car, the victim of the earlier hit and run turned up—and wouldn't you know— the trapped man was the bastard who had run into him and then raced off!

'ARMLESS?

A newspaper delivery man was doing his rounds when he came upon a teenager squatting in front of a cigarette vending machine operated by a local laundry. When asked what he was doing, the unemployed teenager said, 'Trying to steal more cigarettes, but I can't get my arm out'. The delivery man alerted police who then called the fire brigade to rescue the stuck teen. They poured soapy water over his right arm in an attempt to slide it out, but to no avail. When this failed, officers ended up using the key to the machine to open it, releasing the teenager after being trapped for around two hours. Shocked after his ordeal, the teen spontaneously confessed to 43 other unsolved thefts of a similar nature.

GET ME OUT OF HERE!

A not-so-bright young man decided that robbing a bank couldn't be that difficult. So he stormed into a bank menacingly and demanded the teller hand over all her cash. He hadn't figured about security windows. When they began to go up, he realised that his time was short and so he decided to make a run for it. The problem is when he got to the front door it wouldn't open. He pushed it frantically, then shoulder barged it for two minutes, getting more and more desperate. In his desperation he realised that the door had an automatic locking mechanism and he was stuck. As the police arrived on the scene, he sighed and gave up, resigning himself to being arrested. As they escorted him to their waiting car, he noticed a sign on the door in bright red letters that could have saved the day. It said 'PULL'.

JUMP IN MY CAR

An officer sitting in an unmarked car heard reports of a break-in in his area. Moments later, two men dressed in black ran out of the bushes and straight towards him. The men's backs were turned as they got into the car, and they didn't notice his uniform until they were inside. He yelled, 'Police! Freeze!' but they bolted and started running for their lives. But with a police helicopter and tracking units searching for them, they didn't get very far.

HOUDINI HE AIN'T

A man wearing a distinctive red shirt and bright yellow baseball cap held-up a bank and got away with a small amount of money. About 40 minutes later, a police officer walking through a nearby parking lot heard pounding from inside the boot of a car. He opened the boot and—hey presto!—there was a man wearing a distinctive red shirt and yellow cap! It seems the thief had wanted to do a quick change, get out of the boot and head off in a new disguise, but instead he managed to lock himself in. And he was probably hoping that who-ever came to his rescue wasn't a police officer.

STUCK IN THE MUD

When a 36-year-old man got his fire truck stuck in the mud, he did what anyone would do—he used the truck's radio to call for a tow truck. The problem was, the intoxicated man had just stolen the vehi-cle so instead of a tow truck, dispatchers sent the highway patrol to lock him up.

His intentions had been honourable at first, but then it all went wrong. He said he had been on a two-day drinking binge when the clutch of his 1983 Chevrolet gave out. He ended up stuck in the mud on a deserted, winding one-lane street. He didn't know what to do, and not thinking all that clearly, he broke into the nearby fire station looking for a phone. When he couldn't find a phone, he looked around desperately and his eyes fell upon a truck, a small, four-wheel-drive with ladders, water and first-aid equipment. To his beer-muddled mind, his best option was to 'borrow' the truck by driving it straight through the station door. His plan was to use the truck to hitch the car out of the mud, then drive to a payphone to call a tow truck. Unfortunately for him, he bogged the fire truck about 10 metres from his car, called for help, and ended up being arrested. So close and yet so far.

ACCOMPLICES FROM HELL

Stupid sidekicks that let the team down!

There are a lot of impressive dumb crooks out there who work solo, and a lot of other crooks thank their lucky stars for that! You know what they say: two heads are better than one. Two crooks can cover for one another and put up more of a fight, but they also have to share the booty. That can lead to some major brawls. They get narky, turn on each other, and then ...

Bickering crooks have a stupid habit of blowing their cover, usually in a public place like a bar or a pizza joint, where people overhear their conversation or the cops are called in to put a stop to a punch-up and that's when the truth comes out. He did this, she did that! And before you know it, they all end up in jail wishing they'd kept their mouths shut. Let's see what happens when a bunch of stupid crooks get together. The results are often twice as stupid ... which you'd kind of expect, wouldn't you?

GONE SHOPPIN'

A teenager asked his mother to drive him to the bank without telling her he planned to rob it. He told her to wait outside for him. A few minutes later, he came dashing out with the loot, only to find that his mum had gone off to do some grocery shopping

DOMESTIC BRAWL TURNS FERAL

A passerby heard a woman in a van screaming for help and reported it to police. A van matching the vehicle's description was stopped; and sure enough a woman jumped from the van yelling, 'He's going to kill me!' As the police officer went to assist the woman, a large man got out of the driver's seat and approached him in a rather threatening manner. He was arrested and handcuffed after he ignored repeated orders to stop. Then the man and woman got stuck into each other—verbally and physically—and the police officer watched coolly as they basically turned themselves in. Spitting and swearing, she accused him of shoplifting without splitting the goods. He lashed out at her, saying that all she ever stole was cosmetics, and what good were they to him? They even described the bags that contained the stolen goods and showed them to police in their attempts to be as spiteful as possible to each other. And what did it get them? Two prison sentences and a very easy arrest for one police officer.

HEY, WHERE'S MY RIDE?

Three men in a car stopped at a convenience store when one of them said that he wanted to get some beer and cigarettes. What he actually meant was: 'I'm going to steal some beer and cigarettes!' Their friend used a golf club to smash the front doors of the store, grabbed the goods and came out again ... only to find that his mates and the car had gone! Soon after, police found the fellow, drunk, trying to call his friends from a pay phone. Turns out the two men freaked out when they saw him smashing the window and had no idea of his interesting plan.

SLOW DOWN NEXT TIME!

An obsessive master criminal who demanded perfection in every area of his life decided to plan the perfect heist. Every detail was orchestrated to the most minute detail. The bank was chosen after months of research, the time of the robbery was finetuned to the last second, the hiding place for the loot was wickedly clever, and the getaway route was brilliantly planned taking into account traffic lights, peak hour traffic, likely delays, etc. When the plan was finalised, the mastermind behind it all could not have been happier. And so the big day came. The robbery went exactly according to plan and the master criminal fled from the bank, with a bulging sack of money flung over his shoulder. Unfortunately, as he ran towards the rendezvous point, his accomplice ran him over.

IT'S SMART TO CHECK REFERENCES

A gang of bank robbers who had worked together for two very lucrative years planned a series of robberies. At the last minute, one of them broke his leg so they had to hire a new bloke to drive their getaway car. The first break-in didn't quite go to plan. Laden with several bags of loot, the robbers rushed out of the bank towards the waiting car. The new driver panicked and the car stalled. He was still trying to get the car to start as the police arrived. In court, it was revealed that not only did the man not have a driver's licence, but he had never driven a car before.

WRONG DRIVER, BOYS!

Police caught a man sitting behind the wheel of a truck full of stolen auto parts. As he was led away, one of the officers remained behind to impound the truck. He got behind the wheel and started the engine. To his great joy, three guys suddenly appeared from nowhere, jumped into the back of the truck and shouted, 'Let's go!'

SPLITSVILLE!

Two prisoners were handcuffed together on their way to court. They managed to break away and make a run for it. With adrenalin pumping, one ran to the right of a telegraph pole and shouted for the other to follow; the other made for the left of the telegraph pole and yelled back. The result? Some torn ligaments and two broken wrists.

LEGLESS!

Two men hatched a plan to rob an auto parts store. While one talked to a store employee, the other snuck out the back to the manager's office and grabbed $50 cash. The manager put up a fight and a store mechanic joined the melee. In the ensuing scuffle, the store mechanic grabbed the robber's leg and, much to his amazement, it popped off! Apparently, the robber had lost his prosthetic leg—a device which attached below the knee—and when it came loose, it took the thief's pants with it. The victims said they were too stunned to do anything.

Wearing only his boxer shorts, they watched as the man hopped through the snow to his partner's waiting getaway car and off they went. The victims, left holding one unwanted leg, just laughed. They said the entire time he was hopping back to his car he had this look on his face like, 'What should I do?' The thief is really out on a limb—the prosthetic was a titanium, bendable, high-tech device worth several thousand dollars. And the takings from the robbery were $50 split between the two of them. Needless to say, plans are afoot to keep a look out for a suspicious-looking, one-legged, hopping man.

LIGHTS, CAMERA, ACTION!

A drug dealer decided to impress his clientele by hiring a limousine for a big night on the town. His first stop was an upmarket penthouse apartment to do a cocaine deal. Hoping to earn a little extra profit by blackmailing his exceedingly wealthy and influential customer, the crook gave the limo driver a camcorder and asked him to record the event for posterity. The faithful driver was only too happy to oblige—especially since he was a cop moonlighting as a chauffeur.

DON'T FORGET YOUR LUGGAGE!

Four foreigners in Japan entered a Japanese bank. While the female in the group distracted staff by ranting and raving and demanding staff exchange her foreign currency into yen, the three men reached over the counter and stole loot from a cabinet ... a huge haul of over 47 million yen. Fleeing the bank, the four split up, with one jumping on the bullet train with the money. Problem was when he jumped off again, he left the money on the train.

LOOK BEFORE YOU SHOOT

A male was brought in to hospital with a bullet wound to the left side of his neck. He was dropped off and refused all statements at the hospital, however, staff knew that he was a gang member and that his gang was on the prowl that night as there had been a report of a 'drive-by shooting'. Finally all was revealed. The man was a back seat passenger in the car involved. The gunman was also in the back seat. The intended victim happened to be on the other side of the car to the gunman. So the idiot simply shot across the back seat, out the window, forgetting the fact that his buddy was in the seat next to him. The result: one accomplice shot in the neck at very close range. Not knowing what to do but knowing they should do something, they dumped him off at the hospital and high-tailed it out of there.

LEARN TO WRITE, STUPID!

Two would-be robbers who tried to hit a convenience store early Tuesday morning left empty-handed after getting stuck into each other when the shopkeeper didn't understand the threatening note. The two men selected several items and carried them to the checkout counter, then lingered at the back of the store for several minutes before deciding that they would go ahead with the sale. After approaching the counter, one of the men said he needed to get some money from his car and left the store. The second man followed the first man outside. They spent about five minutes in deep discussion before coming back inside. One of the men had a chequebook in his hand and asked for a pen. He then allegedly handed over his chequebook and written on it were the words: 'put it in the bag'. Below the words was another phrase that the shopkeeper couldn't decipher so, genuinely confused, he asked, 'What is this?' The man responded that he didn't know because his buddy had written the note. They then began to argue and left the store, apparently forgetting they had intended to pull a robbery.

JUST CAME FOR MORAL SUPPORT

Two armed men knocked on the door of a house. When the owner came to the door, they went into the 'your-money-or-your-life' routine. The homeowner said he would get the money and closed the door. Why he didn't just lock the door and keep it closed is not clear, but what he did was get a small amount of cash and give it to them. The homeowner by this stage had a pretty good idea of what the thieves looked like. So after they were gone, he called police. One of them got away but they were able to arrest the other based on his description. At his preliminary hearing, the homeowner was asked to identify the defendant by the prosecutor: 'Do you see either of the men who robbed you in court today?' The victim said, 'Yes, one of the men is sitting at the counsel table with his attorney, wearing a grey sweater ... and the other one is sitting over there.' The smart cookie had got away scot-free and what did he do? Drop by at his accomplice's hearing!

THE THREE STOOGES

Three men who broke into a home and shot a man pulled off another trick that left police scratching their heads—somehow, they all ended up shooting one another as they made their escape! A relative had to call emergency crews to come and fetch the men, who had fled the botched home invasion with bullet wounds to the foot, leg, arm and backside. The puzzling thing is that the victim didn't have a gun, so the only guns involved were those of the three crooks. One was shot in the buttocks, one was shot in the hand and foot, and one was shot in the calf. But how they came to manage it, no one seems to know.

NOT ME, STUPID!

A pair of robbers made an impressive debut. They entered a record shop nervously and began waving their revolvers around. The first one shouted, 'Nobody move!' When the second one moved, his partner shot him.

JUST FILL IN YOUR DETAILS

A man and woman robbed a convenience store. While waiting for her boyfriend to finish getting the money, the woman noticed a contest entry form to win a car. Fab, she thought, so she filled out the form complete with name, address and phone number. A few hours later the police showed up at the couple's house ... but it wasn't to congratulate them.

WHO NEEDS MONEY?

I'd rather steal a lobster!

Bank robberies have a certain element of excitement, don't they? Fooling the security system, making your getaway and then hiding your loot in some exotic location. But not all robbers try and hit the big time. Some do and fail pathetically. Other keen crims set their sights a little lower. Instead of cold hard cash, they attempt to steal other things, like fancy dress costumes, live animals or a simple barbecue chicken (try sticking one of those down your jumper!). Most of the time, though, crooks just want the money. But due to tactical errors, they sometimes end up with something much less valuable, like a garbage bag full of dog poo. The following stories are a tribute to petty crims everywhere who throw up their hands, laugh at the world, and say: 'Who needs money ... I'd rather steal a lobster!'

LOOT OR LUNCH?

Two men showed up at a tractor supply store at closing time and demanded the night bank deposit bag. Grabbing a blue bag from one of the employees, they made a run for it. Turns out they went off with the employee's empty lunchbox.

ANYONE FOR SEAFOOD MARINARA?

At 7.30 p.m., diners at a seafood restaurant reported seeing a couple walk out the door. Nothing unusual about that, except that the man left with a live lobster tucked under his shirt. Several witnesses took down the car's numberplate and alerted police to the bizarre seafood theft. The couple, it seems, then got stuck into a huge argument halfway down the street. The man's conscience got the better of him and he wanted to turn himself in, but the woman told him not to be so stupid. Arguing violently, the man drove back to the restaurant to return the lobster. As he got out of the car, his wife grabbed him and a struggle ensued. The restaurant manager came rushing out and the woman grabbed him round the waist, attempting to throw him down. Police arrived soon after and had to crash tackle the woman who was screaming abuse and trying to run away.

I'M ALL LEFT FEET!

A shoe salesman left his hotel one Tuesday morning and found the lock to his pick-up truck had been broken. All his sales samples were gone—312 shoes valued at over $10 000. Funny thing was, they were samples—left shoes only. So, if you've got two left feet, there's a shoe thief somewhere out there with a deal for you.

IT'S NEVER THERE WHEN YOU NEED IT!

Let's say you wanted to spend your day stealing rolls of toilet paper. Where would you do it? Well, a certain man decided the municipal court—always teeming with police officers—was just the place. The man was observed almost daily in the building, even when there were no scheduled hearings. It is estimated that he stole more than 100 rolls over a few months. It was very annoying for the general public and for the cleaner who had to replace the toilet paper countless times. Everyone is now greatly 'relieved' that he was caught.

HOLD THE PEPPERONI

At 2.30 a.m. one Sunday morning, a man rang up to order an extra large vegetarian pizza. He was told that it would take about 30 minutes to arrive, which would seem reasonable to most people, but he found it was just too long. After getting angry about the wait, the customer and the pizza employee started swearing at each other over the phone, and then the man abruptly hung up. Fast forward to 20 minutes later. It's 2.50 a.m and the same guy walks into the pizza joint and orders staff to make him a vegetarian pizza. They're only too happy to oblige, mainly because he has a gun pointed at their heads.

Twenty minutes later—it's now 3.10 a.m. The pizza is ready. What does the armed man do? Grab it and run? Steal all the takings from the till? No. He sits down to enjoy his pizza with a couple of friends who have rocked up with some beer during the hold-up. Luckily for the shaken pizza staff, a delivery driver returning from a job saw this bizarre scenario and escaped to call police.

CLEAN GETAWAY?

A man cased a particular bowling alley and then made plans to steal a regular cash pick-up. Early one Monday morning, he jumped a uniformed delivery truck driver and grabbed a large bag. Turns out the driver was delivering cleaning supplies and the thief scored himself a sparkling range of dishwashing liquid.

BULL!

A thief stole a canister believing it was liquid nitrogen, which is used in the production of methamphetamine. What he actually stole was $4600 worth of frozen bull semen.

... OR ARE YOU JUST REALLY HAPPY TO SEE ME?

Customs officials at LA Airport noticed a man with—ahem—'unusual bulges' around his groin. On closer inspection it was found that he had a veritable menagerie of endangered species stuffed in his underpants. His impressive haul included three socks stuffed with nine dead lizards and three live ones, a Nile monitor lizard, a water monitor, and several South-East Asian geckos.

SURPRISE!

A man was coming out of a shopping centre when he saw a thief hauling two large plastic bags from the back of his ute. He shouted out a warning to him but wasn't too concerned about it. You see, the thief had taken off with about 12 kilograms of dog poo. If the thief stopped to read the side of the van he would have known that it was a pet waste removal company specialising in 'poop scooping'.

NO GOLD STAR FOR YOU

Three men forced their way into a school office at gunpoint and held-up the headmaster and two secretaries. They piled jewellery, money, and the contents of the school safe into a black briefcase, snatched the bag, and ran. Sorry boys, it was the wrong black briefcase ... you got yourselves a bag full of kids' homework.

SOMETHING SMELLS FISHY

A police officer pulled over a car that was weaving down the road. He couldn't help but notice a strong odour and searched the car. The boot was jam-packed with fish—630 trout to be precise. The three men in the car said they'd caught them, but the officer was pretty sure they had stolen them from a nearby trout farm. How did he know? Because every fish was 30 centimetres long!

LOVE THE OUTFIT!

A man decided to siphon some anhydrous ammonia from a tank in a field, which is used in the manufacture of certain illegal drugs. For this, he chose to wear a highly visible pair of bright orange overalls. He also did it in the middle of the day on a busy highway and he unwittingly chose to do this two blocks away from where a major police operation was taking place. With police swarming the area, he was spotted almost immediately. But there's more. In addition to his bright orange outfit, he had taken the precaution of wrapping bread bags around his shoes to waterproof his feet. He thus completely eliminated all forms of effective traction making his pitiful escape attempt laughable. He was quickly cuffed and taken into custody.

Out of interest, this silly person should be grateful police caught him. He was attempting to do the impossible by trying to fill a bucket with pressurised gas. At best, he risked severe injury; at worst a very unpleasant death.

HIT A BIT OF A SNAG

A would-be bank robber went into a bank with a new approach—instead of making a big scene at the front of the bank by holding up the tellers, he went straight for the bank manager's office. He marched in, towered over the manager's desk and demanded he hand over excessive amounts of cash. Before the manager had time to react, the thief's attention was caught by a big bulging bag temptingly within reach. He grabbed it and ran. Didn't he get a big surprise when he opened the bag ... it contained three kilograms of pork sausages.

NO LOAFING!

Wouldn't you know, life is full of intrigue in the bread industry. A certain baker was arrested on charges of burglary, theft of trade secrets, and other related offences stemming from five secret visits to a rival's bakery. Security cameras videotaped the sneaky baker swiping three-ring binders containing 66 recipes used at the long-established family-owned plant, which distributes a wide variety of bread under different brand names across the US. Sadly, the accused baker needs $2 million bail before he'll be making any more dough.

MONEY BAGS?

Two men with a sawn-off shotgun held-up a service station attendant as he walked through a car park just before midnight one night. What attracted their attention was the fact that he was carrying two large dark green bags. The man told them they wouldn't want them, but they took them anyway. They should have listened—the bags were full of garbage.

HIC HIC HIC!

A man thought of an ingenious, if somewhat bizarre, way to get a lot of free alcohol. He hid in a restaurant bathroom until all the employees had left and then he emerged to carry out his fiendish plan. This involved hooking up the beer kegs directly to his mouth. He did this by breaking the door of the cooling mechanism, detaching the hoses leading from the keg, squashing them in his mouth, and literally filling himself up with beer like a pump at a petrol station. Cleaning staff found him the next morning, sprawled on the floor of the restaurant, groggy and totally incoherent but with a big smile on his face.

ALLIGATOR STEW?

'We caught it. We lugged it home across our shoulders. So, what's wrong with having alligator for dinner?' That's what two men told police after witnesses reported seeing them trundling down the road with a live 1.5-metre alligator. Police investigated the matter and found the reports were true. There really was an alligator in their bathroom in a bathtub half full of water. When questioned about it, one of them claimed he found it fishing. The other denied all knowledge of it until his friend pointed out that the alligator's snout was secured with a shoelace that matched the missing shoelace on his right shoe! This particular alligator had a lucky day. The two men were charged with the illegal taking of a protected species, and the alligator was released back into his lake.

WHAT WERE YOU GOING TO DO WITH THAT?

It's very small, portable, valued at about $2500, and it's hard to imagine a more useless thing to steal. A man stole a portable tracking device which, as tracking devices go, automatically alerted police to where it was being taken. 'He apparently didn't know what he had because he would be awfully stupid to steal a tracking device,' said a correctional officer, giving our clever crim the benefit of the doubt. Occasionally low-risk, non-violent offenders are sent home with such devices. The inmates wear a cigarette pack-sized transmitter on their ankle that acts as a 35-metre tether to a portable tracking device. If they wander too far from their device, the jail is alerted. Each battery-powered tracking device has a built-in global positioning system satellite receiver, so it knows where it's located. And each unit is able to transmit its location back to the jail through the Internet. The tracking device that was stolen belonged to a woman who rang the jail and reported it missing. The correctional officer was notified at his home and was able to track the device on his home computer. A trail of electronic dots on his screen followed the clueless criminal as he walked along the city streets and then it stopped. It was then that the police arrived.

LOVE THAT LOOK!

A 22-year-old woman who had just been released from jail apparently really missed her regulation prison wear. She was caught trying to shoplift a prison outfit from a costume hire shop.

HIDE THE BLACK BEAN SAUCE!

Police charged four people in relation to a botched hold-up outside a Chinese restaurant. It's tough to say when the robbery actually started to go wrong—perhaps it was when the gunman started shooting before demanding a wallet or cash? Or maybe when the getaway driver bailed out early? Or perhaps when the robbers made off with their haul—two orders of Chinese takeaway!

Events unfolded when the owner of the Chinese restaurant came out the door and headed for his car with two delivery orders worth about $20 each. As he opened his car door, he heard fast footsteps. He tried to run away but fell over. The men didn't say a word or make any demands; they just starting shooting at him. After firing three shots, the robbers took off with his deliveries, leaving him with a grazed right bicep.

Meanwhile, a friend of theirs, who was the allocated driver for the night, was sitting behind the wheel of his green Ford Mustang getaway car getting more and more nervous. When he heard the shots, he feared the worse and split, leaving his car-less accomplices behind. Without no getaway car, the two robbers took off running. When they were stopped by police and asked what they were doing, they made up a story about being car-jacked. But it didn't add up; both men were out of breath and there was no car on the scene. Then officers found a whole mess of plastic containers and Chinese food spilled nearby and became a tad suspicious. It didn't take them long to arrest the two as suspects in the restaurant robbery.

QUICK KEYBOARD CASH

A musician was looking for some cash, so he decided to steal a keyboard from a nearby church. The church's music director walked into a music store the next day to buy a replacement for the stolen instrument and couldn't believe his eyes when, a few moments later, the crook who stole the keyboard walked in, hoping to sell it to the music store. That particular transaction didn't happen.

MODERN-DAY CLEOPATRA

Tired of essential oils, massages and skin cleanser? One New Age woman was and decided that what she really needed for her mind, body and soul was to bathe in camel's milk. Well, she was a little, shall we say, eccentric. But the obvious question is: Where do you find a camel when you need one? The zoo of course! So with the help of a friend and a hire truck, she managed to 'borrow' a camel from the local zoo in her town. With enormous difficulty, they got it back to her home, only to find that the camel wasn't going to be giving her much milk.

AIRHEADS

Some aircraft employees decided to have a bit of fun on their rostered day off by stealing a large life raft that is used on 747 aircrafts. They went down to the river for a lazy Tuesday afternoon picnic and pumped it up ready to go for a pleasure cruise. Very shortly after, the coastguard arrived on the scene. Our airhead airline employees didn't know that a locator signal had been activated when the raft was inflated.

HENNY PENNY, THE SKY IS FALLING!

A woman calmly walked into a large supermarket and headed for the hot food counter. After checking that no-one was looking, she grabbed a barbecue chicken and shoved it down her jumper. She then proceeded to leave the store, as calmly as she had entered, but she didn't make it—a store detective stopped her and suggested that she was concealing stolen goods. The woman looked absolutely shocked at the very suggestion and even more shocked when a barbecue chicken was produced from under her jumper! She swore the chicken had fallen from the sky and landed in her arms and she stuck to her story until police arrived, sat her down, and showed her the surveillance video.

EAT THEM LATER!

A hungry man broke into a fast food outlet but he didn't want money; he wanted some chips. After grabbing the food, he crossed the road and stood at the bus stop. Police arrived to find a man fitting the exact description of the chip burglar still waiting patiently at the bus stop, still eating chips.

WHY BOTHER?

Two men in a pick-up truck went to a new fully furnished but unoccupied home to steal a large, heavy stainless steel refrigerator. Crashing into walls and denting floors, they struggled and strained but finally managed to load the hulking appliance onto their truck. The truck promptly got stuck in the mud, so these brain surgeons decided that the refrigerator was too heavy. So what did they do? They hoisted it up again and retraced their steps, banging into walls, damaging the floors until finally the refrigerator was back exactly where they had found it! But there's more ... when they got back to the truck, they discovered that they'd locked their keys inside. But did they give up and just go home without the fridge and without their faithful truck? Yes!

THE DEVIL MADE ME DO IT

Dumb crook excuses and stories that just don't add up!

When dumb crooks are caught—which is quite a regular occurrence—they have to prepare themselves for some tough police questioning. Questions like: 'What are you doing here?' 'What is that in your hand?' 'Who is that with you?' Then the questions get even harder and the illogical reasoning and excruciating excuses of our criminal friends range from the sublime to the ridiculous. Deserving full marks for gall, there's the man who couldn't make a court appearance because he pretended that he was dead. Deserving full marks for guile, is the shoplifter who, when asked why he didn't pay for the stolen goods found in his possession, said he didn't realise that he had to! Why do they even bother to explain? Why don't they just say: 'The devil made me do it!'

NICE TRY

A man was stopped by traffic police and issued a ticket for driving alone in the transit lane. The thing is he was driving a mortuary van. So he claimed that the four frozen cadavers in the back should be counted. In a blow for corpses, the judged ruled that passengers must be alive to qualify.

SHE CUT OFF YOUR WHAT ... ?

A man staggered into a hospital one Saturday around 3.00 a.m. with an excruciating story to tell. He was clearly stoned, but he managed to tell staff that he had been the victim of a cruel attack ... a woman had cut off his penis! The story goes that he had brought a woman back to his place and when he made a move on her, she attacked him with a Stanley knife, cutting off his penis and then driving off in a dark blue sedan. Police were called in and he recounted his story. By this time, he was quite delirious. Details of the attack were sketchy, and it was unclear to police why he hadn't been able to defend himself. But still, the man described his mystery attacker in believable detail and he was left to convalesce.

Meanwhile, an extensive police operation sprang into action to trace the vicious vixen, but there were no positive sightings of her. Then on Monday, the man was discharged from hospital. Police were keen to interview him but they could not contact him by phone and he was not at the address he had given them. He seemed to have vanished off the face of the earth.

Police discovered that the man had been involved in the manslaughter of a young woman some years before, so they began to piece together a theory—perhaps the woman who cut off his penis was carrying out a 14-year-old vendetta for the death of her friend? But the truth finally emerged ... After almost two weeks, the man was finally located and brought in for a further interview. It is then that he finally broke down and confessed—he had cut off his own penis! The case was reclassified as an 'injured person report' and the bereft man was charged for filing a false police report. But the mystery still remains—why did he do it?

TRY ANOTHER EXCUSE ...

When he was stopped for going 104 kilometres per hour in a 60 zone, a truckie had a darn good reason—he'd just washed his truck and he was trying to dry it off.

DEVIL'S MUSIC!

A retired police officer decided to carry out his own personal vendetta against crime, and he got away with it for several weeks, until he was reported by one of his victims. What he did was set up illegal speed traps and wait to catch vehicles that had rock music radio station bumper stickers ... because this indicated the driver listened to the devil's music! The bewildered driver was then dragged from the car and had a wet towel placed on his head. When one canny young driver experienced this, he was fairly certain he was not dealing with an authorised member of the police force. So he contacted the 'real' police and, despite his pleas that he was making the highways safer for all decent citizens, our crazy crusader found himself behind bars.

DEFINITELY FROM ANOTHER PLANET

Lawyers are well known for their creative thinking. This one entered a 'not guilty' plea for his client based on astrological forces. He maintained—with a perfectly straight face—that the position of the stars at the time of his client's birth caused him to break into a couple's home, threaten them, tie them up, and walk out with a brassiere on his head.

JUST A PASSING ACQUAINTANCE

At a wedding reception, one man was the life of the party. Rubbing shoulders with everyone, cracking jokes, knowing friends of friends of friends ... then suddenly, everyone noticed he was missing. When he finally returned, more than two and a half hours later, he explained that he'd felt really tired so he'd gone to take a nap. Alas, when the bride and groom reached their apartment late that night, it had been completely done over.

HARD HITTING

A man was held for questioning after allegedly hitting a police officer with a metre-long iron bar. He claimed he was innocent. Simple really, he was just throwing the bar away in case someone tripped over it, when the police officer got in the way!

MY HORMONES MADE ME DO IT!

Police saw a pattern in a recent spate of bank robberies. After investigating three different robberies with the same modus operandi, they were convinced that the suspect was targeting banks in a small locality.

An intriguing factor in the case was that the suspect was always captured on film wearing a heavy winter coat even though it was the middle of summer. Video surveillance footage was circulated and within two days the suspect was recognised standing in a bank queue by two off-duty police officers. When questioned as to why he always wore heavy clothing, he opened his coat to reveal two breasts. Turns out he was an unemployed transsexual who was driven to rob banks to pay for his hormone treatment.

MY EDUCATION MADE ME DO IT!

An unemployed 27-year-old man with an MBA blamed his degree for his failed robbery that resulted in a 10-year prison sentence. 'There are too many business grads out there,' he said. 'If I had chosen another field, all this may not have happened ... '

WELL, THAT EXPLAINS IT!

Stunned witnesses didn't know what to think when they saw a man armed with a machete jump up onto the roof of a police car and lop off the red light. After his arrest, he explained it was 'just something he always wanted to do'.

MR CONFUSED

A naked man was arrested after banging on the door of his neighbour's home at 3.15 a.m. one Sunday morning. He told police that he had drunk 10 beers that night and a taxi had brought him back from a bar to the wrong home. Then his story changed. He said that he had driven himself. Then a friend named Carl drove him home, then another friend drove him home, then his neighbour drove him home. But the neighbour hadn't driven him home—she couldn't stand the sight of him and, anyway, she had been asleep.

Police then tried to get some sense out of him by taking another tack. What about his lack of clothes? His explanation was equally as dodgy. He said that it was a practical joke—a girl had called and asked him to take off his clothes. So he did. But then he changed that story too, saying that a bunch of girls had come by and taken his clothes off. Where were the girls now? They must have run away, he explained. Between the neighbour's vehicle and a flowerbed, the police found all the man's clothes and his wallet. Before being taken to jail, he was allowed to slip into his shorts.

BUDDY, CAN YOU SPARE A TYRE?

A police officer noticed a rental truck crossing several times over the centre line on a highway. Having his suspicions aroused, he stopped the vehicle. The officer talked to both the driver and the passenger and each told a different story as to where they had been and where they were going. The final story was that they were moving one of the men's sister's belongings, except she was not with them. And they were not sure of her name. The officer asked permission to search the truck and found an assortment of furniture thrown into the back—a kitchen table, several chairs, a TV set, and a couple of lamps. Not the way most people pack their sister's furniture when moving. What also caught the police officer's eye was a spare tyre that was way too small for the vehicle they were driving. When he attempted to pick it up, he found that it was unusually heavy and when he thumped it, it made an unusual sound. Not surprising—when the officer cut it open there was 15 kilograms of cocaine inside.

DRIVE MY CAR
INTO A DITCH? WHO ME?

A patrol officer came upon a car in a ditch on the side of the road and found that it had been reported stolen. Residents near the scene told the officer that at about 1.00 a.m. that morning they had heard loud noises. They looked out the window and saw the car in a ditch and someone in the car trying to get out. They described him as tall, skinny and very unsteady on his feet, that is, 'drunk as a skunk'. The crash victim rescued a small white dog from the back of the car and shuffled off down the road. Some time later a man dropped in at the police station—a tall, skinny man to be precise—and, who would've guessed it, he was carrying a small white dog and looking for his 'stolen' car. Police interviewed him for some time before he finally admitted to driving the car into the ditch himself and then reporting it stolen.

IT WAS MY IMAGINARY FRIEND!

Early one morning, a police officer on patrol noticed an old model Dodge pick-up cruising around the same area several times. He followed the vehicle because the driver was operating the truck as if he was intoxicated. As he tailed the truck, the officer also noticed the driver was clearly trying to hide something under the seat. Pulling him over, he asked the driver to show his hands. Instantly the driver stuck his hand out the window and flung out what appeared to be a plastic bag overstuffed with marijuana! The officer impounded the truck, recovered the bag, and informed the driver that he was under arrest for the possession of marijuana. He stared in surprise and asked: 'What marijuana?' At this point the officer replayed the relevant section of his dash cam video that recorded the whole episode, including the part where the driver threw the bag out the window. He watched and then baldly stated, 'That wasn't my arm!'

'Whose arm was it?' asked the patient police officer.

'That's the other guy that was with me.'

And then he unsuccessfully tried to convince the officer that he had a friend hiding under the front seat who had managed to sneak away!

THE MYSTERY PARCEL

Angry that private investigators hired by his ex-wife were going through his garbage, a lawyer sent a large unmarked cardboard box to their office. The box alarmed the private investigators who contacted police. The police, in turn, called in the bomb squad, who blasted open the package ... and found 10 plastic bags of dog poo! The sender was charged with disorderly conduct, but argued that he was only making things easier for the investigators. If they were going to search through his garbage, he thought they'd be pleased to have it sent directly to their doorstep.

TELLING PORKIES!

Two men held-up a deli and made off with a veritable feast including huge amounts of leg ham. One of the men was later tracked down by police. When asked why he had 22 packets of ham under his jacket, he replied that it was for a picnic and that he was just waiting for his mate to come back with the bread rolls.

LIVE IT UP!

A 75-year-old gent must have had quite a dinner party planned. He was arrested for shoplifting two bottles of wine, two packs of shiitake mushrooms, a pack of Portobello mushrooms, four tubs of hummus and some smoked salmon. When asked why he did not pay for the items, he said he didn't realise he had to.

CAN'T MAKE IT—I'M DEAD!

A man who missed a court hearing appeared to have a good excuse, until authorities realised his obituary was a fake, and a paper trail indicated that it wasn't the first time he had pulled such a stunt. In a previous incident, he had faked a heart attack upon arrest.

It all began when a fax arrived at the district court from someone purporting to be the suspect's lawyer. 'Mr X, who I believe is set to stand trial, has recently passed on. Thank you for your time', the fax said succinctly. And a copy of the obituary was included. Instead of dismissing charges against the dead man, the judge added the fax to the court file, because the arresting officer didn't believe it when he heard the news. 'I've never heard of someone faking their own death,' he said, 'but people do come up with some great excuses why they can't make it to court.' While allegedly dead, Mr X seemed to be involved in a number of thefts. When he was finally caught, police thoughtfully had an ambulance on stand-by because of his amazing history of well-timed heart attacks. The suspect was fine until he was told he was going to be arrested. Then a couple of kilometres from the police station, he began to complain of chest pains. Hey presto!, an ambulance materialised and the poor man was taken to hospital. The prognosis? Nothing wrong with him. And what did our prone-to-heart-attacks hero do when confronted with the fake obituary? He simply feigned surprise at how reports of his death came to be so wildly exaggerated.

UGLY, SMELLY AND SORE FEET

A man's short-lived career as a thief began one fateful morning, when he walked seven blocks from his apartment to a bank, carrying a small bag. He threatened to detonate a bomb unless the teller handed over $100. His 'explosive', police later learned, was a can of cold beer. The teller handed over the cash and triggered a silent alarm. Bizarrely, officers arrived as he was leaving, but didn't detain him, so he walked down the block to the next bank he found. Same modus operandi, same beer can and another $100—not bad for 20 minutes' work. He then ambled over to a park about 20 metres away and plopped down on a grassy patch to rest his weary feet in full view of an officer quizzing a witness!

Standing outside the bank, an officer asked a female witness for a description. She looked over, did a double-take, and said, 'That's him!' All that was left was for the police officer to walk over and place him in custody. Later down at the station, under questioning, the man revealed his motive for the robberies, 'I'm ugly and I smell bad and I can't get a job. So I gotta get money somehow'. He may blame his looks and body odour, but it was his sore feet that did him in.

JURY DUTY HAS NEVER BEEN SO GOOD

Many people see being called up for jury duty as a hassle. But one man saw it as a golden opportunity to get six months' paid leave, courtesy of taxpayers. What happened was this: he was summoned to jury duty but the court wound up not needing him. Despite this, he told his bosses that he was required to serve on a very complex case that could potentially last for several months. They accepted what he said and he couldn't believe his luck—a nice little income and no work!

To keep up the charade he would drop by his office from time to time to pick up his pay slips, always rushing in and explaining that he was on a break and needed to get back to jury duty. After several weeks of this, his supervisor asked for some proof of jury service and he promised to provide it. His supervisor asked again a week later, and he assured her that proof was coming. A week later he resigned.

His company investigated and a check with the courthouse revealed that he never served a single day on the jury. He was arrested and charged with grand theft and official misconduct by falsely claiming to be on federal jury duty for six months. Even though he collected $17 388.47 in pay during that time, he didn't come out of it a winner.

I JUST LOVE PAYING
MY RENT IN ADVANCE

Two builders were renovating an elderly woman's house when they found a once-in-a-lifetime discovery in her attic—no less than $90 000 cash. It was just too tempting, so they stole it. But then one of them did a pretty stupid thing. Feeling wealthy, he decided that with his share of the money he would pay off a year's worth of his rent. So he went to his landlord with the cash. Most landlords would be a little suspicious if a tenant came with $50 000, willing to pay for a year's rent in advance. This landlord was particularly suspicious ... because he was a cop! Police obtained a search warrant and recovered the $90 000 from the man's house. And the poor woman was greatly relieved to get her money back.

HANDY HINTS

Tips from the experts to set you off on the wrong track!

Here are some ideas to keep in mind next time you are contemplating getting out your ski mask and water pistol. All these tips have been gleaned from real-life scenarios and just go to prove that dumb crooks make the world a more fascinating place.

HANDY HINT 1

If you are on jury duty, don't do drug deals on your lunchbreak—you will probably be seen. As was the case with a 50-year-old juror who was found during her lunchbreak doing deals at a nearby café, carrying 181 packets of heroin with an estimated street value of $4000.

HANDY HINT 2

If you are up in court charged with reckless driving, try to think up something a little more convincing then, 'Your Honour, there are extenuating circumstances. I only crashed because I was up late the night before making counterfeit cheques.'

HANDY HINT 3

If you're a bank robber fleeing from the US into Canada there are three things you should do: lose your gun; lose your blonde woman's wig; and get rid of your robbery hold-up note. A suspected bank robber had all three items with him in his vehicle as he tried to cross the border. He didn't make it.

HANDY HINT 4

If you're planning to leave the country with $25 000 worth of designer label clothing that you have just shoplifted, don't arrive at the departures desk with excess luggage in the form of eight bulging suitcases ... you may stand out in the crowd and customs officials may well be interested in what is in them!

HANDY HINT 5

If you decide to escape from prison by climbing out a window using sheets tied together to form a rope, figure out where you will land before you reach the ground, otherwise you may end up on a prison courtyard where guards are having their mid-morning break. And secondly, if you are using the above strategy with some mates, don't send the fattest one down the sheets first ... he will rip them and you will not achieve your freedom!

HANDY HINT 6

If you're the kind of idiot that sells drugs, don't hand out your personal business card. It makes you kinda easy to track down! Two dodos were arrested after a man gave police a business card he had been given on which the obliging dealer had supplied his name, phone number and an attractive picture of a marijuana leaf.

HANDY HINT 7

Take care when there are police dogs about, as one woman learnt when she was arrested at her Boy's Scout meeting. She was watching a police officer demonstrate his sniffer dog's ability ... and you guessed it, it came right up to her, gave her purse a good sniff, and uncovered a bag of marijuana.

HANDY HINT 8

If you're going to write a hold-up note and hand it to a teller, make sure it's legible; unlike the teenage girl who attempted an armed robbery that went badly wrong. The teller couldn't decipher the writing on her hold-up note and had to pass it to another teller. And then a third teller came over to try and read it. By the time the teen was handed a bag of money, it was almost closing time, employees were locking the doors, and the failed bank robber got trapped between double doors in the foyer.

HANDY HINT 9

When you've robbed a bank, don't go back to the same branch the next day. And especially don't try to open an account ... someone will recognise you!

HANDY HINT 10

If you're planning to rob a bank, take your iron tablets at breakfast time. Don't be like the anaemic bank robber who went into a bank, held-up the teller at gunpoint, demanded money, and before she could answer, fainted. Police arrived to find the failed bandit still lying unconscious on the floor.

HANDY HINT 11

If you need a hold-up note for your next bank robbery, don't write it on the back of your résumé. One smart fellow did just that, but (cleverly) tried to disguise it by sticking black tape over the back. He didn't realise that police could peel off sticky tape.

HANDY HINT 12

If you are planning to hold-up a café, shop or bank at gunpoint, check for the presence of police and police cars first. And if you see any, don't carry out your crime, at least not until they go away! Unlike the unobservant young man who held-up a café, failing to notice the four marked police cars in the café parking lot. Or the six armed police officers all having coffee inside.

HANDY HINT 13

If you want to be a successful armed robber, don't let your victim go into a bank alone to cash a cheque for you. Unless they are as stupid as you are, they will not come back!

HANDY HINT 14

If you're going to rob a bank, don't pick one that is still under construction. Unlike the man who marched into his local branch and demanded $500 from the tellers, telling them he had a gun. The tellers told the would-be robber that the bank was not yet open for business and thus, had no money. The man promptly turned and walked out of the building, right into the hands of the police.

HANDY HINT 15

After you rob a bank, run away. Don't be like a certain robber who was discovered moments after the robbery, crouched down behind a car in the bank car park, counting his loot.

HANDY HINT 16

If you're going to rob a motel, make sure there isn't a Police Law Enforcement Training Conference being held there. One thief failed to read the banner across the lobby welcoming police officers to the conference and was subsequently shocked when his robbery didn't quite go according to plan.

HANDY HINT 17

Don't flee the scene of the crime on a bright pink bicycle. People will notice you!

HANDY HINT 18

Don't put on your mask before you leave home; police will spot you driving to your selected hold-up site, and they will follow you and catch you!

HANDY HINT 19

Try and wear a mask that covers your face. Unlike the bright spark who realised he didn't have a disguise, so once inside the shop he grabbed a clear plastic bag and pulled it over his head. Apart from almost suffocating, it didn't hide his face at all!

HANDY HINT 20

Don't wear a bright orange Hawaiian shirt when you rob a convenience store. Security camera video captures your fashion choice—and when it's shown on national TV, someone is bound to recognise you!

HANDY HINT 21

Don't wear pyjamas when robbing a bank, especially red ones with little yellow stars and moons on them. People will notice you in a crowd, watch what you do, and will be able to give police nice helpful clues as to your whereabouts!

HANDY HINT 22

If you rob a bank, don't go out to celebrate at the restaurant next door to the bank. Bank employees may well see you and remember what you have done!

HANDY HINT 23

After you have held-up a bank, don't ask the teller to call you a taxi. This is what one bright spark did who clearly didn't have a brilliant exit strategy in place.

HANDY HINT 24

If you're using a getaway car, make sure it's not terribly noticeable. Unlike the hapless bunch of bank robbers who chose to get away in the only maroon-coloured Edsel registered in the entire state of Nebraska!

HANDY HINT 25

Don't use a van emblazoned with your business name and phone number when you attempt a hold-up. A plumber tried it twice and was arrested at the scene of a third robbery when his van matched the descriptions from witnesses at all three stores. As the arresting officer said, 'He made it pretty easy by advertising himself.'

HANDY HINT 26

If you're going to steal a car, get a good night's sleep the night before. Unlike one soporific sneak who was found by police in a compromising position snoozing in a stolen car with the motor running, head resting on a suspicious bag of white powder.

HANDY HINT 27

If you are going to rob a sandwich shop, don't take a bite of a sandwich while you're there—you may end up like the crook who couldn't resist a bite of a meatloaf sandwich as he dashed out the door. The cops ran a DNA test on it and—bingo!—they found a match to a meatloaf-loving crook who had just been jailed (again) on another burglary charge.

HANDY HINT 28

If you're breaking into someone's apartment, remember that you're supposed to scare them; they're not supposed to scare you. Unlike the cat burglar who was walking on the balcony of an apartment at 12.30 a.m. one morning when he knocked over a very large pot plant. The young couple who were asleep instantly woke up and the man yelled out to the intruder, who was so shocked at the sudden noise, that he toppled over the balcony railing onto the balcony of the unit below.

HANDY HINT 29

If you're going to steal $50 000 worth of computers from your high school, don't try to sell them on e-Bay. When the computers were stolen from his classroom, a high school teacher figured that e-Bay was the obvious place to look but he didn't believe that anyone would be stupid enough to think they could get away with it anonymously. Well, two 18-year-old students were that stupid!